WE MUST PRAY THE SCRIPTURES

The Life-Changing Power of Praying God's Word Over Every Area of Your Life

Ramatu Allen

We Must Pray The Scriptures: *The Life-Changing Power of Praying God's Word Over Every Area of Your Life*

Published by Kingdom Renewal Press
Ohio, United States

ISBN: 979-8-9958117-1-8

Scripture quotations are taken from the Holy Bible, New International Version® (NIV®).
Copyright © 1973, 1978, 1984, 2011 by Biblica, Inc.™
Used by permission. All rights reserved worldwide.

Printed in the United States of America

First Edition 2025

DEDICATION

I dedicate this book to my loving husband and three sons, who are my joy, my teachers, and a constant reminder of God's faithfulness.

May your hearts always be strong in the Lord, your steps steady in His truth, and your lives filled with His purpose. I pray over you now and always that you will be men of strength, wisdom, and unshakable faith.

To my family and friends, your love, prayers, and support have been a gift to me, and I'm forever grateful.

And to the readers, thank you for accepting the invitation to prayer. I pray that this book becomes a guide as part of your time spent with God.

PREFACE

Dear Reader,

Thank you for picking up this book and opening your heart to the sacred work of prayer. I don't take it lightly that you're here. There are many things you could be reading, many places your time could go, but you've chosen to pause and enter into the presence of God. What a beautiful decision.

Prayer is one of the greatest gifts we've received, and yet we often neglect it. Life pulls on us from every direction, especially for those of us caring for homes, raising children, building marriages, and trying to serve others well. But prayer? Prayer brings us back to center.

As a wife and a mother, I have learned that the secret place is not a luxury; it's my lifeline. Prayer has carried me through exhaustion and joy, disappointment and hope, moments of quiet, and seasons of chaos. When I've had no words, the Spirit has interceded. When I've felt too overwhelmed to know what to pray, I've turned to Scripture, and God has met me there every single time.

This book was born out of my own journey of learning to pray the Word of God through every area of life, not just in crises but in the quiet dailiness of being a woman after God's heart. I've written it the way I'd speak with a friend over coffee, with warmth and honesty. You won't find perfection here, just encouragement, simplicity, and a whole lot of Scripture.

I hope this book is a gentle companion on your journey, reminding you that you're never alone, that the Father hears you, and that praying the Scriptures is one of the best things you can do for your heart, home, and future. Let's pray together.
With love and grace,
Ramatu Allen

How to Use This Book as a Daily Prayer Guide

This book is more than something to read—it is a companion for prayer on your journey as a follower of Jesus Christ. Each page is designed to help you cover your life and the lives of your loved ones in prayers. You can go through it section by section or skip to the section that fits your needs for the season.

Here are some simple ways to make the most of this book:

Daily Reading & Reflection

- Begin each day with the opening scripture from the section you're focusing on.

- Read the teaching to connect your heart to God's truth for that section.

Pray the Prayer

- Speak the written prayer aloud or silently.

- Personalize it by adding names, specific needs, or circumstances you're facing.

- Don't worry about "perfect words"—God hears and knows your heart.

Journaling Your Journey

- Use the journaling prompts for deeper reflection.

- Be honest and specific—your journal can become a testimony of God's faithfulness in your life.

Carry Hope With You

- Declare the scripture and prayers boldly over your life and situations in Section Three until they become part of your daily rhythm.
- Write the declarations on a Post-it note or index card and tape it where you can see it; choose one per week and declare it until it becomes true in your mind and heart.

Repeat & Return

- Come back to the chapters that align with your current stage of life. Read it, pray over it, meditate on it, and devote some time to applying it.

- Use section three to quickly find verses and prayers for specific needs such as surrender, healing, strength, or protection.

Remember: Prayer is not about taking control; it is about surrender. As you pray daily, you are entrusting your life and worries to the One who knows, loves, and cares for you deeply and wants nothing more than receiving your request, your worship, and spending time with you daily.

Table of Contents

Section 3: A Heart Set on Prayer: Scripture-Prayer for Every Season of Life.

Introduction

You Can Talk to God Right Where You Are

I want to begin by telling you something you might need to hear today:

You don't have to be perfect to pray.

You don't need big words, long sentences, or a special setting.

You just need a willing heart.

God is near, right where you are. Whether you're sitting with this book in a quiet moment or reading between errands and responsibilities, He's here. He's not waiting for you to clean up, calm down, or catch up. He's simply waiting for you to come.

I believe that prayer is one of the most powerful things we can do. But I also know how easy it is to feel overwhelmed by it. Maybe you've asked:

- Am I doing it right?

- What do I even say?

- Is God really listening?

- How can I pray when my heart feels numb?

Friend, I've been there. And I want to assure you, prayer doesn't have to be complicated to be meaningful. It's simply a conversation with your Heavenly Father, one that grows over time.

This book was written to walk with you, not preach at you. Think of it like a quiet chat between friends, one mom, wife, or believer in Christ to another, sharing what it means to lean on the Lord through prayer.

Each chapter is designed to help you grow in prayer using the Word of God as your foundation. This is because the Word of God consistently provides the answers we need when we need them.

You'll also find simple prayers, Scriptures to speak aloud, and journal prompts to help you reflect and pray through what's going on in your heart and home. Don't rush. Take your time. Reread chapters if you need to. You are welcome to skip around to sections that align with your needs. There's no wrong way to walk with God.

Whether you're just beginning your prayer journey or you're longing for a fresh start, this is your invitation:

Come as you are, and pray through everything.

He's listening. And He loves you more than you can imagine.

Let's begin.

Section One

Foundations of Prayer

Why We Must Pray

"You do not have because you do not ask God."
— James 4:2b, NIV

Have you ever prayed and felt like your words were bouncing off the ceiling? You're not alone. Many believers love God deeply but struggle with unanswered prayers. The good news is this: God has already given us the key—His Word.

Some days, prayer comes easily. Words flow, tears fall, and faith rises. Other days, it feels hard. We're dry, distracted, and distant. Life often pulls us in a hundred directions, often pushing prayer to the back of our priorities list. We love God, but if we're honest, we sometimes live as if we can manage without Him.

But we can't. We were never meant to.

I was only 27 years old when I first became a single mother. I worked a full-time job and had a somewhat decent income. But with childcare, food, rent, healthcare, etc., my income was never enough to cover rent and keep food on the table, and sometimes I was so stressed I could not find the strength to face another day.

I didn't have anyone to lean on, no safety net, no backup plan. Prayer was all I had.

But through those whispered, tear-soaked prayers, I realized that God was my provider. He carried me through nights of fear and mornings of exhaustion. That season taught me that prayer wasn't optional; it was survival.

Prayer isn't just something we *do*—it's how we live. It's how we breathe. How we stay grounded. It's how we bring heaven into the midst of our daily mess.

When scripture tells us to "pray without ceasing" (1 Thess. 5:17), it's not about performance; it's about closeness. The enemy loves a prayerless Christian.

If the enemy succeeds in keeping us occupied, resentful, burdened, and too distracted to pray effectively, we will try to confront life's challenges relying on our own strength.

And, my friend, relying solely on your own strength will wear you out.

Jesus Prayed—and He Was the Son of God

Even Jesus, the Son of God and Savior of the world, made time to pray. Luke 5:16 says, *"But Jesus often withdrew to lonely places and prayed."*

He needed time alone with His Father, not just in moments of public ministry but in quiet and chaos alike. If He needed that connection, how much more do we?

Why Does Prayer Matter?

Prayer is how we:

- Hear God's heart

- Receive peace in our minds

- Invite His power into our weakness

- Align our will with His Word

Through prayer, we experience grace, favor, strength, and healing—things we could never produce on our own.

James 5:16 reminds us, *"The prayer of a righteous person is powerful and effective."*

You may not always feel powerful or righteous. But if you belong to Jesus, His righteousness covers you, and your prayers matter more than you realize.

Don't Let Guilt or Distraction Silence You

Many times people stop praying because they feel like they've failed at it. They missed a few days. They got distracted. They fell asleep mid-prayer (yes, me too).

I'll never forget a season in my banking career when life was full of pressure to perform, deadlines, and endless to-do lists, while I was overwhelmed at home, raising two sons as a single mother. On the outside, I appeared successful, but on the inside, I was exhausted. I often skipped prayer, convincing myself I was "too busy." But the more I neglected time with God, the heavier I felt.

I was doing everything in my own strength, and it nearly broke me. One morning, desperate and worn down, I finally cried out to God during my commute.

That fifteen-minute prayer in the car gave me more peace than months of striving ever could. It was a reminder that the enemy wins when I stay prayerless, but victory comes when I return to God with even the simplest prayers.

But prayer isn't about perfection. It's about a relationship. It's about honesty. It's about opening the door again and again and saying, *"Lord, I'm here."*

No matter how long it's been, He welcomes you back without shame.

A Word of Encouragement From a Sister Still Learning

There have been times when prayer was the only thing that kept me standing. When I had no words, I whispered a verse. When all I could do was cry, I sat in silence—and God met me there.

Growing up in Liberia taught me what it means to lean on God. Life wasn't easy. Resources were few, opportunities were scarce, and the future felt uncertain. I remember walking down streets filled with struggle, yet I also saw people who prayed with unshakable faith. I didn't fully get it at the time, but their trust in Jesus made a lasting mark on me.

Years later, when I moved to the United States, I gave my life to Christ. But even before I fully surrendered, I found myself drawn to prayer. In moments of homesickness, financial stress, or fear of failure, I would pray—and somehow, even without knowing Him deeply yet, God gave me peace and strength to keep going.

Now, as a wife and mom, I can clearly see how prayer has been the thread holding my life together.

Every major decision, every hard season, every new beginning—prayer has been at the center.

So if you're in a hard place right now… If you're tired. If you're worried about your family. If you don't know what to say. Even if you're not sure about Jesus yet. If you're carrying burdens no one else knows about—hear me: God is ready for you. You can come to Him just as you are. He's not afraid of your questions, your fears, or your struggles. He will meet you right where you are.

Prayer

Father, thank You that I don't need to have my life all together to come before You. Your Word says, *"You do not have because you do not ask God"* (James 4:2). So today, I choose to ask.

I choose to pray, not just when I feel strong, but especially when I feel weak, because *"the prayer of a righteous person is powerful and effective."* According to James 5:16.

You promised in Jeremiah 29:12, *"Then you will call on me and come and pray to me, and I will listen to you."* So I call on You now, Lord. Please teach me to draw near to You in every season.

Give me the grace to run to You instead of away from You. Remind me daily that You hear me, that my prayers matter, and that You are near.

I surrender my striving, and I choose to pray. I want to know more about you. Please help me start right here and now. In Jesus' name, Amen.

Declaration:

I declare that I am a person of prayer. God hears me when I call, and my prayers are powerful. I will not rely on my strength—I will lean on the Lord daily.

Journal With Jesus

1. What's been holding me back from praying more freely?

2. What area of my life do I need to surrender in prayer today?

3. What would it look like to treat prayer as a lifeline, not just a task?

Praying for God's Presence

"My presence will go with you, and I will give you rest." —Exodus 33:14, NIV

There are days when your heart is full and prayer flows like water.

And then there are days when you're just trying to make it to bedtime without breaking down.

On both days, and all the ones in between, God wants to be with you.

His presence isn't reserved for Sunday services or early-morning devotionals. His presence is for laundry rooms, waiting rooms, school pickup lines, and grocery store aisles. He's not watching you from a distance. He wants to walk with you through every part of your real, messy, beautiful life.

Prayer Is More Than a Moment—It's a Mindset

We often think of prayer as something we "schedule." Yes, dedicated time with God matters, but prayer is more than a slot on your to-do list.

Prayer is awareness.
Prayer is an invitation.
Prayer is walking through life with your Father's presence woven into everything you do.

God isn't waiting for perfect silence to meet with you. He whispers in car rides, stirs your heart while you fold towels, and wraps peace around you while you wash dishes.

When I was a young mother working full-time, I used to think I could only meet with God during early-morning devotions. But with little sleep and a full schedule, those moments felt impossible. One day, while washing dishes, I whispered, *"Lord, I need You here."* The peace that settled over me was so real, I realized I didn't need a set hour to find Him—I needed an open heart.

That moment taught me that His presence is not bound by time or location.

How Do We Become More Aware of His Presence?

We can become more aware of His presence by inviting Him into our everyday lives.

- "Lord, walk with me today as I parent."

- "Holy Spirit, speak through me in this meeting."

- "Jesus, give me strength as I make this meal."

- "Father, sit with me while I rest."

These prayers don't have to be long. But they change everything.

Think of Joseph in Genesis. Whether he was in Potiphar's house, in prison, or in Pharaoh's palace, the Bible repeats a simple truth: *"The Lord was with Joseph."* (Gen. 39:2, 21). God's presence wasn't limited to holy places. It followed Joseph into his work, his suffering, and his success.

The same is true for you—His presence can saturate every season of your life.

A Life Saturated in Prayer

In Psalm 16:8, David said, *"I keep my eyes always on the Lord. With him at my right hand, I will not be shaken."*

Can you picture that? Imagine having God by your side in every situation, whether it's in the kitchen, the hospital room, the classroom, or the office.

His presence giving you strength when you're tired, gentleness when you're irritated, and peace when you're overwhelmed.

That's what it means to live a life saturated in prayer—not a perfect life, but a present one.

Imagine carrying your phone everywhere without ever turning it on. The power is there, but it remains unused until you connect by turning the phone on. God's presence is like that—always available, always near. Prayer is the way we "turn on" our awareness and stay connected throughout the day.

You Can Be a Woman (or Man) Who Walks With God

Not just someone who prays when there's a crisis. Not just someone who says they trust God.

But someone who builds their life around His nearness.

And when the world feels loud, rushed, and chaotic, His presence will be the quiet place your soul can return to again and again.

When I first launched my business, I often felt overwhelmed by all the responsibilities.

I would usually work on my business after work; often I would check my emails and direct messages and respond at the same time I was making dinner.

I remember one particular afternoon when my toddler was crying for no other reason than just to be held, and I had a pile of clients' direct messages and emails to respond to because I had just started promoting a new product.

At that moment, I became so overwhelmed that I didn't know what to do.

In that instant, I whispered, "Holy Spirit, please help me now." Suddenly, a calm came over me. I got through that evening with peace I knew wasn't my own. God reminded me that His presence isn't just for ministry moments—it's for motherhood, work deadlines, and everyday chaos, even the little moments too.

Prayer

Holy Spirit, thank you for living in me. The word of God says, *"My Presence will go with you, and I will give you rest"* (Exodus 33:14).

You are my helper, my comforter, and my constant friend. Lord Jesus, You promised, *"Surely I am with you always, to the very end of the age"* (Matthew 28:20).

I invite you into my prayer life today. When I feel distracted or discouraged, remind me of Psalm 16:11: *"You make known to me the path of life; You will fill me with joy in Your presence."* Teach me to listen for Your voice. Bring Your Word to my remembrance and guide me into all truth.

Fill my mind with peace, my heart with joy, and my spirit with strength. I surrender this moment to You. In Jesus' name, Amen.

Declaration:

I declare that God's presence goes with me today. I am never alone. His peace surrounds me, His Spirit strengthens me, and His love sustains me.

Journal With Jesus

1. When have I felt the Holy Spirit's help in my life, even in small ways?

2. What distractions or fears do I need to surrender to the Holy Spirit today?

3. What would it look like to let Him lead my prayers instead of rushing through them?

The Power of Praying the Scriptures

"Your word is a lamp for my feet, a light on my path." —Psalm 119:105, NIV

What if I told you that the words you say in prayer can shift the atmosphere, stop the enemy, and move mountains? That is the strength of praying God's Word; it always works.

I understand that prayer isn't always easy. It can feel as though you are forcing yourself to express just a few words. But here's the truth: even if you're just learning to pray, you can grow stronger and more confident in your prayer walk. How? You can achieve this by praying the Scriptures.

His promises are more than just comforting thoughts; they are a place where you can find peace, hope, healing, love, salvation, and so much more. The scriptures become your solid base for your prayer.

When I first gave my life to Christ, I thought prayer meant long, emotional sessions of begging God for help.

Sometimes I'd cry so hard, only to walk away feeling defeated because nothing seemed to change, and I was even angry with God at times.

I couldn't understand why my prayers weren't being answered or why my situations weren't changing, and I didn't even know what to ask for anymore.

Then one day, I was listening to a teaching from the late Kenneth Hagin, and he was discussing getting your prayers answered by praying the word of God back to him.

That day I discovered the power of praying scripture—instead of saying, *"Lord, please do this,"* I learned to say, *"Lord, You said in Your Word..."* I learned and realized that prayer wasn't about persuading God but about aligning with His promises. This realization became the foundation of my prayer life and the driving force behind the creation of this book.

The late Kenneth Hagin explained that praying the scriptures aligns you with the will of God; it causes you to see how much he loves you and cares about your problem.

Life won't always make sense, and we can't rely on our feelings. What we want today may not be what we need or be good for us.

But God's word is not based on our feelings. **God's promises become your power when you pray them; your will becomes aligned with his.**

Praying the Scriptures helps you shift your focus away from your complaints, personal concerns, and worries, allowing you to concentrate on God's will, and that brings you peace.

John 14:27 says, *"Peace I leave with you; my peace I give you... Do not let your hearts be troubled."* That's a promise.

So when you're feeling anxious or unsure of what to pray, you **don't have to invent perfect words**. You can speak the perfect Word that's already written in the Bible.

Through the word of God, you learn who he is and all his promises for you, giving you hope and peace.

He helped me see that hoping, wishing, crying, and begging didn't move God; it was prayer that came with the word of God that moved him. This is due to the fact that the word of God serves as the foundation for your faith, which is derived from its abiding presence within you.

If you remain in me and my words remain in you, ask whatever you wish, and it will be done for you. -John 15:7

God's word builds faith; His word is His will, and praying for His will to be done creates answered prayers.

So I opened my Bible.

I started praying God's words back to Him. At first, it felt a little awkward, almost like I was just reading aloud. But the more I did it, the more I sensed his presence. I wasn't searching for perfect words anymore. I was standing on His promises.

There have been many times in my life when I've felt homesick, out of place, and at times invisible. During my struggles and feelings of lack as a new believer, I often didn't know what to pray, how to ask God for help, or what the right words were to say.

In those moments, I would open my Bible to Psalms and pray David's words as if they were my own: *"The Lord is my shepherd; I lack nothing."* That Scripture became my lifeline.

I wasn't just reading; I was speaking life into my fear, reminding myself that God was with me in an unfamiliar land.

Although I wasn't sure if I was praying correctly and often doubted whether my prayers were reaching heaven, I found that my desires were fulfilled countless times, even when I lacked the right words to express them in prayer.

God knows the desires of our hearts; praying his word back to him when we don't know what to say is oftentimes the only thing you need to do to have your prayer answered.
There's another reason to pray the Word: **because the enemy hates it**. He will try to distract you, discourage you, and whisper lies. He'll tell you you're too sinful, too far gone, or that your prayers are not long enough to be heard by God.

But Romans 8:38–39 crushes that lie:
 "Nothing… shall be able to separate us from the love of God that is in Christ Jesus our Lord."

When you pray the Scriptures, you silence the enemy. You remind your spirit who you are and who your God is.

God's Word Never Comes Back Empty

When Jesus faced the devil in the wilderness, He didn't argue. He didn't cry. He didn't beg. He said three words: 'It is written.' That same authority is available to you when you pray the Word of God.

There was a time when I felt like my words were small compared to the size of my problems. I would pray, but my prayers felt empty, like I was just talking into the air.

But the moment I began declaring God's Word—verses like Isaiah 55:11, *"So is My word that goes out from My mouth: It will not return to me empty"*—things shifted. I realized I wasn't just speaking; I was releasing God's authority into the atmosphere. That revelation gave me boldness to pray with confidence, even in the hardest seasons of my life.

Scripture isn't just for studying; it's for speaking, declaring, and standing on. When we pray Scripture, we're praying truth, not just feelings.

We're anchoring our hearts in what God has already spoken, and we trust Him to do what only He can do.

So, Why Pray the Scriptures?

- Because sometimes you don't know what to say.

- Our words may falter, but God's will is unwavering.

- The enemy does not back down when we cry or beg, but he flees when we speak the truth of God's Word with authority.

- God's word never returns void; it always accomplishes its purpose.

It Doesn't Have to Be Complicated

You don't need a theology degree to pray the Bible.

Here's how it might sound:

- *Lord, Psalm 23 says, 'You are my Shepherd. I lack nothing. Please provide for me today.*

- *God, Your word says in Philippians 4:6, 'Do not be anxious about anything, but in every situation by prayer and petition, with thanksgiving, present your requests to God.' Therefore, Lord, I give you my worries. Replace my anxiety with Your peace.*

- *Father, You said I don't have to fear because You are with me. Strengthen me now according to your word in Isaiah 41:10.*

- *Lord, I feel anxious today, but I know that I am more than a conqueror through Him who loved me," According to Romans 8:37, so thank you for covering me with your peace today. I have overcome, and I win in Jesus' name.*

See how simple that is? You read it. You receive it. You speak it. These are not just verses. They are **weapons.**

And when you do, you are praying powerfully.

If it is promised, it's his will; he's already told us his will in the scriptures. He has given us the authority to use his word and proclaim his will. And when you pray this way, you are taking the burden off yourself to have control and placing it on God through his word, giving God control over your life.

During a period in my years working in banking, I faced pressure to perform, meet sales goals, and juggle clients' expectations. There were days when I was crushed by stress and anxiety.

I began writing verses on sticky notes and placing them on my desk. Before meetings, I would quietly pray Philippians 4:6–7: "Do *not be anxious about anything... and the peace of God... will guard your hearts and minds in Christ Jesus."*

Even in that fast-paced environment, God's Word steadied me. My coworkers saw peace on me when I should have been falling apart; that was the power of praying Scripture.

Faith Comes by Hearing

Romans 10:17 says, "Faith *comes from hearing the message, and the message is heard through the word about Christ.*" The more you speak God's Word—even softly, even while driving or cooking dinner—the more your faith will rise. You're not just reading it. You're hearing it. And your spirit begins to catch hold of it.

You Can Start Today

You don't have to be in crisis to pray the Scriptures. You can do it while washing the dishes, before picking up the kids, or while lying in bed at night.

Pick a Psalm. Start with a promise. Write a verse on a sticky note and whisper it when fear tries to creep in.

It doesn't have to be fancy. It just has to be real.

God's Word in your mouth is a sword in your hand.

As a wife, mother, and businesswoman, I often need new courage. When I start to worry about money or being a good mom, I remember God's promises. I've prayed Isaiah 41:10 countless times over my business decisions: *"So do not fear, for I am with you... I will strengthen you and help you."*

Those words have carried me through launching courses, running a business, and even staying up all night with a toddler. When I say them out loud, it's like having a shield against worry.

The battle is not yours—it's the Lord's. But you fight it by opening your mouth and declaring His Word. You are backed by the promises of God and the power of His Spirit.

When life shakes you, speak the unshakable Word.

When doubt attacks you, declare what God has already said.

When fear rises up, remind it of who your Father is.

Because praying Scripture is more than spiritual discipline—it's spiritual victory.

Prayer

Dear God, thank you for your word—steady, true, and powerful. *"Your Word is a lamp to my feet and a light on my path"* (Psalm 119:105). When I don't know what to say, remind me that Your promises are already written for me.

You declared in Isaiah 55:11 that *"so is My Word that goes out from My mouth: it will not return to Me empty, but will accomplish what I desire and achieve the purpose for which I sent it."*

Teach me to pray scripture in my everyday life, to hold it in my heart, and to speak it with confidence when I feel fearful, weak, or unsure.

Jesus, You said in John 15:7, *"If you remain in Me and My words remain in you, ask whatever you wish, and it will be done for you."* Anchor me in Your Word so my prayers align with Your will. Strengthen my trust in You today.
In Jesus' name, Amen.

Declaration:

I declare that the Word of God is alive in me. I pray with power and authority because His truth lives in my heart. My faith is growing, and my prayers align with His will.

Journal With Jesus

1. What's one Scripture I want to start praying daily?

2. How does it feel to pray God's Word instead of trying to "figure out" what to say?

3. Where in my life does the truth of Scripture need to take precedence over my feelings?

Inviting the Holy Spirit

"And I will ask the Father, and he will give you another advocate to help you and be with you forever—the Spirit of truth."
—John 14:16–17a, NIV

You're not praying alone.

Even when it seems quiet, you are not alone in your prayers. Even when the words won't come. Even when your thoughts wander or your heart is heavy, you are not alone.

The Holy Spirit is with you. And He's not just beside you... He's in you.

Jesus knew we would need help to pray. He knew our human minds would grow tired and our hearts would sometimes feel stuck. So He gave us a gift: the Holy Spirit, our Comforter, our Helper, our constant Guide.

You Don't Have to Do This in Your Own Strength

Romans 8:26 says, *"In the same way, the Spirit helps us in our weakness. We do not know what we ought to pray for, but the Spirit himself intercedes for us through wordless groans."*

Isn't that a relief?

You don't have to come up with a perfect prayer. You don't have to feel strong. You don't have to pretend.

When you don't know what to say, the Holy Spirit steps in. He takes your sighs, your tears, and your silence—and lifts them to the Father with power and love.
I will never forget my first year as a single mother. I was exhausted, overwhelmed, and terrified of what the future would hold for me and my child. Most nights, I couldn't find the words to pray.

I would sit at the edge of my bed, tears streaming down my face, softly whispering only the word "Jesus." And in that silence, I felt the Holy Spirit carry my cries to the Father.

It wasn't very eloquent, but it was real, and God heard me. That season taught me that prayer isn't about performance; it's about presence.

What Does It Mean to "Invite" Him?

The Holy Spirit is always present. But there's something powerful that happens when you welcome Him into the moment.

It's as simple as saying:

- "Holy Spirit, help me pray."

- "Lead me right now."

- "Give me the words."

- "Fill this room with Your peace."

You don't have to beg or perform. Just invite.

And as you do, you'll begin to sense a shift, a quiet strength, a calming presence, and a spiritual clarity that can only come from Him.

He Reminds You What's True

Jesus said in John 14:26:

> *"But the Advocate, the Holy Spirit, whom the Father will send in my name, will teach you all things and will remind you of everything I have said to you."*

That's what the Holy Spirit does. He brings Scripture back to your mind. He helps you remember what God has promised. He gently nudges your heart when you've drifted. He convicts—not to shame but to restore.

You Can Talk to Him

You don't have to wait for a church service or a special moment. You can speak to the Holy Spirit in the kitchen, in the car, while folding laundry, or right before you fall asleep.

You can say:

- "Holy Spirit, comfort me."

- "Strengthen me to walk in love."

- "Help me forgive."

- "Give me wisdom before this conversation."

And He will. Because He's not just God's Spirit—He's God's gift to you.

Let Him Lead

The Holy Spirit will never lead you into confusion or chaos. He brings peace. He brings clarity. He always points you to Jesus. As you grow in prayer, remember this: **you are not in this by yourself.**

During my first year of marriage, there were many times when misunderstandings made communication with my husband difficult. Instead of rushing to argue or shut down, I started asking the Holy Spirit to guide my words.

One evening, after a particularly tense day, I prayed in the kitchen, "Holy Spirit, please give me the words that bring peace, not division." That small prayer shifted everything. Our conversation that night ended not in anger but in reconciliation. The Spirit led me, and He'll lead you too.

Prayer

Holy Spirit, thank you for being my Helper, my Advocate, and my Guide. Jesus promised in John 14:16–17: *"I will ask the Father, and He will give you another Advocate to help you and be with you forever—the Spirit of truth."*

When I don't know what to pray, I trust Your Word in Romans 8:26: *"The Spirit helps us in our weakness. We do not know what we ought to pray for, but the Spirit Himself intercedes for us through wordless groans."* Please intercede for me when I lack the words to pray. Speak truth to my heart, align my desires with God's will, and help me walk in step with You daily.

Lord Jesus, You promised in John 14:26 that *"the Holy Spirit will teach you all things and remind you of everything I have said to you."* Remind me of Your truth, fill my home with Your presence, and lead me into obedience. I surrender every part of my life to You. In Jesus' name, Amen.

Declaration:

I declare that the Holy Spirit lives in me and leads me. I am never without help. He gives me wisdom, peace, and power to pray according to God's will.

Journal With Jesus

1. When have I felt the Holy Spirit's help in my life, even in small ways?

2. What distractions or fears do I need to surrender to the Holy Spirit today?

3. What would it look like to let Him lead my prayers instead of rushing through them?

Aligning Your Prayers With the Will of God

"This is the confidence we have in approaching God: that if we ask anything according to his will, he hears us." —1 John 5:14, NIV

Have you ever cried out to God until your voice was hoarse—yet nothing seemed to change? I've been there. The breakthrough isn't in how loud we cry but in aligning our prayers with the Word of God.

Sometimes, when prayers go unanswered, we quietly wonder:

- *Did I say the wrong thing?*

- *Did I ask for too much?*

- *Is God even listening?*

Those are real questions. And if you've ever asked them, you're not alone. The truth is God is listening. He always hears the cries of His children. But His answers are shaped by something deeper than our desires:

His will

And that's not something to fear. That's something to trust.

God's Will Isn't Against You—It's For You

Sometimes we hear "God's will" and assume it means we won't get what we want. But God's will isn't cold or distant. His will is good, it's pleasing, and it's perfect (Romans 12:2). It's the path that leads to peace, not pain. It's rooted in His wisdom and not in our emotions.

When we pray in alignment with His will, we're not shrinking our prayers; we're strengthening them.

We're saying, *"God, I trust that what You want for me is better than what I can see right now."*

Think about Hannah in 1 Samuel 1. She prayed desperately for a son. For years, nothing happened. But in her waiting, her prayer shifted from personal longing to kingdom purpose: *"Lord Almighty, if you will only look on your servant's misery… then I will give him to the Lord for all the days of his life."* (v. 11).

God answered her prayers. Samuel was born and he became a prophet who shaped Israel's destiny.

When Hannah aligned her prayers with God's greater plan, heaven moved.

Jesus Gave Us the Example.

In Luke 22:42, Jesus prayed, *"Father, if you are willing, take this cup from me; yet not my will, but yours be done."*

Even Jesus, in the Garden of Gethsemane, felt the tension between His desire and the Father's will. He asked honestly. But He surrendered fully.

That's the balance we learn to walk in as people of prayer, bringing our requests boldly but surrendering the outcome to a faithful God.

As a single mother, I prayed often for God to "fix everything quickly"—the finances, the loneliness, the uncertainty. But his answers rarely came on my timetable.

Looking back, I see how he used those seasons to build my faith, teach me resilience, and prepare me for marriage and ministry later. What felt like unanswered prayers were actually training grounds. His will was shaping me, even when I didn't understand.

How Do I Know If I'm Praying God's Will?

One of the simplest ways is this:

If your prayer lines up with His Word, you can trust it lines up with His will.

That's why praying Scripture is so powerful—because God has already told us what he desires, and they include:

- Healing

- Forgiveness

- Wisdom

- Peace

- Salvation

- Restoration

- Fruitfulness

- Justice

- Grace

When you pray for those things, you're not guessing—you're agreeing with heaven.

Think of it like signing your name to a check. If I write an amount on a check without having the authority to do so, the bank won't honor it.

And I might even end up in jail for signing a check I had no authority to sign.

However, if someone with the appropriate accounts and authority signs the check, it holds significant weight. When you pray God's Word, you're signing your prayers with His authority. Heaven recognizes it—not because of your name, but because of His.

But What About the Prayers He Hasn't Answered?

There will be moments where you pray in faith... and wait. Moments where you ask with tears... and nothing changes—yet. In those moments, let your heart rest in this truth:

God's "No" is Never Rejection; It's Redirection

He's not denying you out of punishment—he's protecting you, guiding you, and growing you.

Sometimes the waiting is the answer.
Sometimes He's building something in you before He brings something to you.
And sometimes... He's just saying, *"Trust Me."*

Through my corporate banking career, I have prayed for certain promotions that never came.

At the time, it felt like God was silent. But years later, I saw how He was redirecting me—away from positions that would have consumed me and toward my true calling.

During the COVID season, God provided me with the opportunity to work from home in a position for which I was barely qualified if it weren't for his grace. My regional manager believed in my ability to learn on the job and got me connected to a team that worked in another city over two hours away from me.

I was nervous because this position was not one I had prayed for, but almost five years later, I have been able to work from home consistently.

I have been able to take my children to school in the morning, pick them up afterward, and use the time saved from traffic to work on my skills and develop myself as an author, coach, and entrepreneur.

I've had the chance to work with the best team and managers, who have supported me in prayer and love during my hardest times. What looked like delay was actually divine protection.

Don't Be Afraid to Ask—Just Be Willing to Surrender

Ask for big things. Dream big dreams. Cry out in faith.

But then open your hands and pray, *"Lord, Your will—not mine. I trust You with the outcome."*

That kind of prayer moves mountains and molds hearts.

Prayer

Heavenly Father, thank you that your will is good, pleasing, and perfect according to Romans 12:2. Your Word says, *"This is the confidence we have... If we ask anything according to Your will, You hear us"* (1 John 5:14). So I come boldly, yet surrendered, praying, "Your kingdom come, Your will be done on earth as it is in heaven" (Matthew 6:10).

I declare Romans 12:2 over my mind. Renew my mind with Your word, oh God, so my desires reflect Yours. Teach me to trust You with outcomes I can't control (Proverbs 3:5–6).

Shape what I want until it mirrors what You want; delight my heart in You and align my petitions to Your purposes according to Your will (Psalm 37:4). I let go of my striving and choose to rest in Your sovereignty. In Jesus' name, Amen.

Declaration:

I declare that God's will is better than my own. I trust His timing, His plan, and His heart. My prayers are aligned with heaven, and I receive the peace that comes from surrender.

Journal With Jesus

1. Is there a prayer I've been holding tightly that I need to surrender today?

2. In which areas should I consider replacing frustration with trust?

3. What's one Scripture that reminds me of God's will and promises?

Section Two

Praying Through Real Life

When Prayer Feels Hard

Praying through Resentment, Offense & Torment

"The Lord is close to the brokenhearted and saves
those who are crushed in spirit."
—Psalm 34:18, NIV

What do you do when your prayers feel like they
bounce off the ceiling? What do you do in those
moments when prayer feels heavy?

When your lips may whisper a prayer, but your
heart feels distant... guarded... worn out?

You love God. You believe in Him. But part of you
is tired. Maybe even a little angry.

Maybe you've carried the weight of prayers that
went unanswered, people who hurt you, or
situations that didn't turn out the way you hoped.
Maybe you're still carrying them now.

If that's you, let me remind you:

- Prayer is still for you.

- God still hears you.

- You are still welcome at His feet.

God Isn't Afraid of Your Honesty

You don't have to put on a brave face when you pray. He already sees behind it anyway.

- When Hannah was overwhelmed, she prayed *"in bitterness of soul, weeping bitterly"* (1 Samuel 1:10).

- When David was angry and afraid, he poured it out to God in the Psalms.

- When Job was tormented, he questioned and cried, but he never let go of faith.

Your father is not offended by your emotions. He loves you too much to let resentment, offense, or torment settle in your soul.

Bitterness Blocks the Flow

For a season, I struggled with unanswered prayers and couldn't understand why. Then God gently showed me areas of unforgiveness, fear, and doubt that were blocking my prayers.

It was humbling, but it was freeing.

Matthew 6:14 says, *"If you forgive others when they sin against you, your heavenly Father will also forgive you."*

I realized that holding on to offense was like putting a wall between me and God. I felt a weight lift when I decided to forgive and let go. I was able to pray more freely, and I started to get answers that had been delayed for years.

When we hold on to resentment or offense, it's like trying to pray through a closed door.

Jesus taught this lesson clearly: *"And when you stand praying, if you hold anything against anyone, forgive them, so that your Father in heaven may forgive you your sins."* (Mark 11:25)

Forgiveness doesn't mean pretending it didn't hurt. It means releasing what you were never meant to carry and letting God carry you instead.

Sometimes, we must let go of our bitterness before we can get the breakthrough we want in prayer.

Think of a clogged drain. No matter how much clean water you pour in, it won't flow until the blockage is cleared. In the same way, unforgiveness clogs the flow of peace in our hearts.

Once forgiveness is released, prayer flows freely again.

There were also times in my marriage when I carried unspoken resentment. I would pray for God to fix things but still hold on to silent offense in my heart. It wasn't easy, but I learned to forgive in prayer, even when I didn't "feel" like it, and things shifted.

God softened my heart, healed old wounds, and brought peace into our home. Prayer became lighter once I let go of the weight.

Torment Can't Stay Where Peace Is Welcome

Maybe what you're facing isn't resentment but torment—spiritual heaviness, mental pressure, emotional turmoil.

Friend, God doesn't want you to stay in torment. His Word promises peace: *"Now may the Lord of peace himself give you peace at all times and in every way."* (2 Thessalonians 3:16)

This is especially true when your soul is experiencing torment. Even if your voice shakes, start praying the Word out loud. It makes no difference if you can only recite one verse.

Remember to pray even if your words are overshadowed by your tears. When you pray Scripture, the enemy cannot stay; he will flee.

In 1 Samuel 30, David returned to find his city burned, his family taken, and his people ready to stone him. The torment was real. But the Bible says, "David *strengthened himself in the Lord his God*" (v. 6). He didn't deny the pain—but he turned to prayer, and God restored all he had lost.

Healing Starts with One Honest Prayer

You don't have to fix it all today. You don't have to heal overnight. You just have to be willing to start talking to God again.

Pray something as simple as:

"Lord, I'm hurt. I'm tired. I'm angry. I don't even know how to pray right now. But I'm showing up. And I want to trust You again."

That one honest prayer can open the door to healing, and He will meet you there.

Prayer

Lord, Your Word says in Psalm 34:18, *"The Lord is close to the brokenhearted and saves those who are crushed in spirit."* I declare that You are near to me in my brokenness. I decree that I am not alone, for You are saving and strengthening me in my weakness.

As it is written in 1 Peter 5:7, *"Cast all your anxiety on him because he cares for you,"* I declare that I cast every weight, every anxious thought, and every hidden hurt onto You. I decree that my burdens are lifted because You care for me.

Your son taught in Mark 11:25, *"When you stand praying, if you hold anything against anyone, forgive them, so that your Father in heaven may forgive you your sins."*

By Your grace, I choose forgiveness. I decree that offense and bitterness will not rule my heart, and I release those who hurt me into Your hands.

According to Ephesians 4:31–32, *"Get rid of all bitterness, rage and anger... Be kind and compassionate to one another, forgiving each other, just as in Christ God forgave you,"* I declare that anger and bitterness are removed from me. I decree that I am clothed with kindness, compassion, and forgiveness.

As it is written in Philippians 4:7, *"The peace of God, which transcends all understanding, will guard your hearts and your minds in Christ Jesus."* I decree that Your peace guards my heart and mind right now. I declare healing from the inside out, and I receive wholeness in the name of Jesus.

In Jesus' name, Amen.

Declaration:

I declare that I am free from torment and bitterness. The peace of God fills my heart. I release offense and choose forgiveness. Healing is mine because God is near to the brokenhearted.

Journal With Jesus

1. What emotion have I been holding that I need to release to God today?

2. Is there someone I need to forgive—even if they never say sorry?

3. What do I want to say to God that I've been holding back?

Forgiveness and the Power of Having a Clean Heart When Praying

---

"If we confess our sins, he is faithful and just and will forgive us our sins and purify us from all unrighteousness." —1 John 1:9, NIV

Sometimes what stops us from praying or being fully present during our prayer times isn't time, tiredness, or distractions. Sometimes, it's the weight we're still carrying in our hearts.

- We carry guilt that we refuse to release.

- We harbor bitterness and refuse to forgive.

- We hide our resentment behind busy schedules and polite smiles.

These things don't just affect our emotions—they affect our ability to pray freely.

Because the truth is...
Unforgiveness clutters the soul.

You Can Come Clean—Without Fear

Shame makes us feel far from God, even when He hasn't moved. Guilt convinces us we're not worthy of speaking.

But here's what the Word of God says:

> "Therefore, there is now no condemnation for those who are in Christ Jesus." —Romans 8:1, NIV

God isn't looking for a perfect prayer. He's looking for an honest heart.

He already knows what's there: the secret shame, the unspoken anger, and the quiet disappointments you've buried. And He's not holding it over your head. He's holding out His hand.

When you bring it to Him, He doesn't scold you. He cleanses you. Not partially. Not conditionally. **Fully.**

David knew this well. After his greatest failure, adultery, deception, and guilt, he didn't hide from God. Instead, he prayed, *"Create in me a pure heart, O God, and renew a steadfast spirit within me."* (Psalm 51:10).

God forgave him, restored him, and still called him a man after His own heart.

That's the power of confession and cleansing, not that we've done everything right, but that we run to the only One who can make it right.

Forgiving Others Frees You

Unforgiveness doesn't hurt the person who wronged you. It hurts you—your spirit, your joy, and even your prayers.

Jesus said in Matthew 6:14–15: *"For if you forgive other people when they sin against you, your heavenly Father will also forgive you. But if you do not forgive others their sins, your Father will not forgive your sins."*

Those are strong words, not to shame us but to free us. This is because forgiveness allows us to remain free.

Forgiveness was one of the hardest lessons for me. I held on to anger for years toward people who hurt me deeply. For years, I carried the weight of my mother's absence; growing up, my stepmother's harsh discipline; and my father's unpredictable temper.

I thought about every birthday that went unnoticed, every milestone with no one there to cheer, and the long, quiet nights when I longed for a mother's comfort.

I told myself I would one day confront my mother and make her feel the pain I had lived with.

Later, in counseling, my therapist asked me a question that changed everything: *"Would you prefer to be free or to be right?"* That pierced my heart. I realized my anger was costing me more than it was punishing her.

As I began to forgive, not in one moment but in repeated choices, I felt lighter.

When I had completely forgiven, my soul felt free. That forgiveness didn't erase the past—it freed my future. Forgiving didn't mean excusing what was done, but it did mean releasing the weight to God.

Think of your heart like a garden. Bitterness is like a weed. At first, it's small—barely noticeable.

But left alone, it spreads fast, choking out the flowers and fruit you've planted. Forgiveness is the act of pulling the weed out by its roots so your garden can grow again.

Forgiveness also helped me learn how to set boundaries. It didn't mean excusing harmful behaviors or pretending everything was fine.

It meant choosing peace, setting healthy limits, and keeping my heart safe while still extending grace. By forgiving others, I was freeing myself from the burden of resentment.

You're One Honest Prayer Away From a Fresh Start

Whether it's shame from your past or hurt from someone else's actions—you don't have to carry it one more day.

Lay it down in prayer.
Allow God to clean the slate.
Let your heart breathe again.

There is so much more on the other side of forgiveness.

Prayer

Dear Heavenly Father, I come honestly before You, confessing my sins and my need for You. Your Word says in 1 John 1:9, *"If we confess our sins, He is faithful and just and will forgive us our sins and purify us from all unrighteousness."*

I declare that as I confess, You forgive me and cleanse me. I decree that unrighteousness is removed from my life because of Your faithfulness.

As it is written in Psalm 51:10, *"Create in me a clean heart, O God, and renew a steadfast spirit within me."* I declare that You are renewing me from the inside out. I decree that my heart is purified and my spirit is made steadfast through Your power.

According to Matthew 6:14, *"For if you forgive other people when they sin against you, your heavenly Father will also forgive you."* Lord, I choose to forgive, and I declare that I also walk in Your forgiveness.

Psalm 103:12 says, *"As far as the east is from the west, so far has He removed our transgressions from us."* I declare and decree that my sins are no longer counted against me. I declare that I am free because of Your mercy.

According to 2 Corinthians 5:17, *"If anyone is in Christ, the new creation has come: The old has gone, the new is here!"*

I declare that I am a new creation in Christ. I decree that the old is gone, and I now walk in the mercy, freedom, and new life You have given me.

In Jesus' name, Amen.

Declaration:

I declare that my heart is clean and free. I am forgiven, and I forgive others. Nothing will hinder my prayers. God's grace renews me daily, and His love sets me free.

Journal With Jesus

1. Is there anything I've been afraid to confess to God? Why?

2. Who do I need to forgive so my heart can be free?

3. What would it feel like to truly believe I'm forgiven and walk like it?

Choosing Gratitude

"Give thanks in all circumstances, for this is God's
will for you in Christ Jesus."
—1 Thessalonians 5:18, NIV

Gratitude doesn't always come naturally.

Some days it flows easily—when prayers are
answered, when blessings are visible, when joy
feels close.

But what about the days when nothing seems to
change?
When you're still waiting?
When your heart grows weary and your faith
begins to wane?

That's where chosen gratitude begins.

It's not the gratitude that comes from everything
being perfect. It's the kind that rises up even in
uncertainty and says, *"God, You are still good."*

Gratitude Shifts Your Perspective

Thanksgiving doesn't deny your struggles—it reframes them.

Philippians 4:6 tells us: *"Do not be anxious about anything, but in every situation, by prayer and petition, with thanksgiving, present your requests to God."*

Did you catch that? *With thanksgiving.*

That means gratitude isn't something we tack on after God answers. Gratitude walks into the waiting room with us.

- God is still good.

- God is still near.

- God is still working, even when I can't see it.

Paul and Silas embodied this in Acts 16. Beaten, chained, and thrown into prison, they chose to sing hymns and pray with thanksgiving. Their gratitude in a dark place unlocked a miracle—the prison doors flew open. Gratitude didn't just change their mood; it changed the atmosphere.

Gratitude Opens the Door to Peace

The very next verse in Philippians says: *"And the peace of God, which transcends all understanding, will guard your hearts and your minds in Christ Jesus."* (Phil. 4:7)

Peace doesn't come from control. It comes from trust.

When you whisper *"thank you"* in the middle of pain, you're letting go and saying, *"God, I trust You anyway."*

I'm grateful for the breath in my lungs.
Even for strength to face today.
I am grateful for the lessons I didn't want to learn but found were necessary.

Sometimes, gratitude doesn't feel easy; I recall periods when practicing gratitude felt impossible.

When I was a single mother, I often saw more bills than blessings. And more often than not, I felt abandoned by God, so saying "thank you" was harder. But I learned to start small. *"Thank you, Lord, for waking me up. Thank you for my children's smiles. Thank you that I'm not alone."*

Those small thank-yous became seeds of hope. And no, gratitude didn't erase my struggles, but it gave me eyes to see God's hand holding me through those times.

Gratitude Softens Hard Seasons

Our life experience is a mix of joyful and painful chapters. Gratitude doesn't erase the hard parts, but it helps us view various situations in those chapters as part of a bigger picture, allowing us to recognize the good things amidst the bad or difficult experiences, which in turn helps us focus on the positive times and build our strength and resilience.

Psalm 107:1 declares, *"Give thanks to the Lord, for he is good; his love endures forever."*

Gratitude is how we keep our hearts tender and our eyes open to see His goodness even in dark valleys.

Gratitude is like turning on a light switch in a dim room. The furniture doesn't change—the challenges are still there. But suddenly you can see clearly, move safely, and rest more easily. Gratitude doesn't change the facts; it changes your perspective.

Start Small; Stay Consistent

If gratitude feels like a stretch right now, start small:

- Thank you for breath.

- Thank you for your word.

- Thank you for never letting go.

- Thank you for walking with me through this moment.

Before long, those small thank-yous begin to shift the atmosphere of your prayers and your heart.

When I launched my first business, stress often overshadowed my joy. I kept a notebook by my bed where I wrote three things I was grateful for each night. Some days it was big, like a new client or a breakthrough idea. Other days it was simple, like a good meal, laughter with my kids, or a moment of peace. That habit changed me. Gratitude became the lens I saw my life through, and it turned worry into worship.

Prayer

Lord, thank You that even when life feels messy and I don't have all the answers, You are still good. Teach me to come to You with thanksgiving in every prayer.

Your Word says in Isaiah 40:31, *"But those who hope in the Lord will renew their strength. They will soar on wings like eagles; they will run and not grow weary; they will walk and not be faint."*

I declare that as I wait upon You, my strength is renewed. I decree that I will rise up like an eagle, I will run and not grow weary, and I will walk and not faint, because You sustain me.

The word of God declares in Psalm 28:7, *"The Lord is my strength and my shield; my heart trusts in him, and he helps me. My heart leaps for joy, and with my song I praise him."*

I stand firm on your word and I decree that You, Lord, are my strength and shield. I declare that my heart trusts in You fully, and therefore I rejoice and give You thanks.

Open my eyes to see what You are doing, even in the small things. Thank You for never leaving me. Thank You for always being enough.

In Jesus' name, Amen.

Declaration:

I declare that I will give thanks in every circumstance. Gratitude is my posture, and joy is my portion. I see God's goodness all around me—even in the waiting.

Journal With Jesus

1. What am I grateful for today, even if it feels small?

2. How has God shown His goodness in my life lately?

3. What would change in my prayer life if I made gratitude my starting place?

Praying for Strength

"But he said to me, 'My grace is sufficient for you, for my power is made perfect in weakness."
—2 Corinthians 12:9, NIV

Let's be honest—sometimes it feels easier to scroll Instagram than to sit in God's presence. Distractions are one of the enemy's favorite weapons to keep us powerless in prayer.

Some days, strength feels out of reach.

You love your people, but you're tired.
You trust God, but you're overwhelmed.
You keep showing up, but inside, you feel like you're barely holding it together.

If that's where you are today, hear this: **you don't have to be strong all the time.**

Because your strength was never meant to come from you.

Strength Isn't About Having It All Together

We live in a world that says, "*Be strong. Push through. Don't let them see you break.*"

But God says something very different:

> "Come to me, all you who are weary
> and burdened, and I will give you rest."
> —Matthew 11:28, NIV

The strength God gives doesn't come from striving. It comes from surrender.

It's in the coming to Him—honest, tired, and tear-streaked—that we finally discover the strength we've been trying to fake on our own.

Think of Elijah in 1 Kings 19. After a massive victory over the prophets of Baal, he collapsed under a broom tree and prayed to die. He was exhausted, empty, and done. God didn't scold him. Instead, He sent an angel with food and water and let Elijah rest. Only then did God strengthen him to keep going.

True strength often begins with admitting we are weak.

His Strength Shows Up Best in Your Weakness

Paul, who wrote much of the New Testament, prayed three times for God to take away his "thorn"—some kind of weakness or trial.

But instead of removing it, God gave him this promise:

> "My grace is sufficient for you, for my power is made perfect in weakness."
> —2 Corinthians 12:9, NIV

Think about that.

God doesn't just work *despite* your weakness—He works *through* it.

That means you can stop pretending.
You can stop hiding your struggle.
You can stop thinking you're disqualified just because you're tired.

There have been days I've felt so drained—physically, emotionally, and spiritually—that I wondered how I would make it through.

As a wife, mom of three, and someone carrying multiple responsibilities, exhaustion sometimes feels constant.

But Isaiah 40:31 became a lifeline: *"Those who hope in the Lord will renew their strength. They will soar on wings like eagles."*

I began to pray that scripture over myself.

I didn't always wake up with superhuman energy, but I noticed that God gave me strength for each day, just enough to keep going. Looking back, I see that His strength carried me in seasons when mine ran out and is still carrying me today.

Strength Doesn't Always Look Like You Expect

Sometimes, God gives us strength in unexpected ways.

Sometimes he gives it through rest. Sometimes it comes through a friend's encouragement, a quiet moment in His presence, or a single verse that lifts your soul.

Remember, Isaiah 40:31 promises:

"But those who hope in the Lord will renew their strength.
They will soar on wings like eagles;
They will run and not grow weary;
They will walk and not be faint."

Your job isn't to create strength.
Your job is to hope in the Lord and let Him renew you.

Think of your phone battery. It doesn't recharge itself; it has to be connected to a power source.

You can drain it to zero, but once it's plugged in, it comes back to life. In the same way, we don't generate strength on our own—we "plug in" to God, our true source of power.

A Simple Prayer for the Weary Heart

Sometimes all you can say is, *"God, I need You."*

That's enough.

He's not asking you to be superhuman. He's asking you to come to Him with empty hands and an open heart and let His strength carry you where yours runs out.

Prayer

Lord, I am tired. I have tried to be strong, but today I need Your strength more than ever. Thank You that I don't have to hold everything together, because Your power is made perfect in my weakness.

As it is written in Philippians 4:13, *"I can do all things through Christ who strengthens me."* I declare that my strength is not my own, but it comes from Christ within me. I decree that I am upheld by the Lord, and I can endure, overcome, and move forward through His power.

Fill me with strength that comes from heaven—not from pressure, not from pride, but from Your peace. I decree that I will lean on You instead of trying to carry everything alone. I declare that today I walk in Your strength, and I trust You to carry me through.

In Jesus' name, Amen.

Declaration:

I declare that the Lord is my strength and my song. I do not rely on my own power—I lean on God. His grace sustains me, His Spirit strengthens me, and His rest restores me.

Journal With Jesus

1. What part of my life feels the heaviest right now?

2. Where have I been relying on my own strength instead of God's?

3. What does "leaning on the Lord" look like for me today, in a practical way?

Praying for God's Guidance and Wisdom

"If any of you lacks wisdom, you should ask God, who gives generously to all without finding fault, and it will be given to you." —James 1:5, NIV

There are many decisions we have to make in life. Some are small, like deciding what to make for dinner. Others are life-altering, like which career path to choose, how to deal with problems in our marriages, or how to make health decisions concerning our families.

And in those moments, the questions rise:

- *What should I do?*

- *Is this God speaking... or just me?*

- *What if I choose wrong?*

If you've ever prayed through these questions, you're not alone.

The good news is you ***don't have to figure it out alone.***

Wisdom Is for Everyone

Sometimes we think God only gives guidance to the spiritually "elite." But James 1:5 tells us plainly: anyone who asks can receive.

That means wisdom is available for:

- The tired mom who feels stretched too thin.

- The student choosing between schools.

- The husband who is enduring a challenging phase in his marriage.

- The believer, yearning to obey God but who is uncertain about how to discern His voice.

If that's you, you don't have to beg. You just have to ask.

Think of Solomon in 1 Kings 3. When God offered him anything, Solomon didn't ask for riches or power. He asked for wisdom. And God gave him wisdom so great that leaders from around the world sought his counsel. That's the heart of our Father—He delights in giving wisdom when we ask.

God's Will Isn't a Maze

We often treat God's will like a hidden map we could miss if we make the wrong turn. But Scripture paints a different picture:

> "Whether you turn to the right or to the left, your ears will hear a voice behind you, saying, 'This is the way; walk in it.'" —Isaiah 30:21, NIV

God isn't playing hide-and-seek with your future. He desires to lead you in a step-by-step manner, guided by your prayers.

And even when you're uncertain, He is still guiding.

I can't count how many times I've faced decisions where I felt completely lost—whether in parenting, finances, or ministry.

In those moments, I wished that God would just send me a text message with the answer. But God does not work like that; he already told us in his word, in James 1:5: *If any of you lacks wisdom, you should ask God, who gives generously to all without finding fault.*

I started asking in faith and then waited for His direction. Sometimes His wisdom came through scripture, other times through wise counsel, and often through a gentle nudge in my spirit. Learning to pause and seek His wisdom has saved me from many mistakes.

What Does God's Guidance Look Like?

God's guidance doesn't always come in the form of a loud voice. Often, it's a gentle nudge. God can lead through:

- You may find a Scripture that resonates deeply within your heart.

- You might experience a sudden sense of peace or discomfort regarding a decision.

- Wise counsel from a trusted believer.

- A door that opens… or one that closes.

- A peaceful assurance that you're on the right path.

God leads with peace, not panic. God leads with clarity, not confusion.

A simple prayer for discernment could be:

- "Lord, if this is from you, let it grow. If it's not, let it fade."

- "God, lead me with your peace. Don't let me go where you're not."

Think of God's guidance like a GPS. If you miss a turn, the system doesn't shut down—it simply recalculates to get you back on track. In the same way, God's Spirit can redirect you if you step off course.

His goal isn't to trap you in fear but to lead you forward with grace.

Don't Be Afraid to Wait

Sometimes God's clearest direction is: *"Wait."*

And waiting isn't punishment. It's protection. It's preparation. It's positioning.

While you wait, keep praying. Keep listening. Keep reading His Word. He is never late. His timing is perfect.

Think of the Israelites in Exodus. God led them with a cloud by day and fire by night. Sometimes they stayed put for days; other times for months. They only moved when God moved.

Waiting was part of their obedience—and part of their guidance.

I became extremely overwhelmed in a season in my job; I prayed for clarity about whether to stay or step out into something new. For years, it felt like no clear answer came.

Looking back, I realize that season of waiting was God's way of preparing me. By the time he opened the door to my new position, I had gotten the position I loved, a team I adored, and the opportunity to work from home—more than what I asked for or even imagined. His "not yet" was really His way of saying, *"Trust My timing."*

Prayer

Lord, You see the decisions before me—the ones that feel overwhelming and the ones I am afraid to make. Thanks for guiding me, so I don't have to figure everything out alone.

Your Word says in James 1:5, *"If any of you lacks wisdom, you should ask God, who gives generously to all without finding fault, and it will be given to you."*

Father, I've come to ask for your wisdom. I decree that confusion must bow to Your clarity and that You will speak to me in ways I can understand.

Proverbs 3:5–6 says, *"Trust in the Lord with all your heart and lean not on your own understanding; in all your ways submit to him, and he will make your paths straight."* I declare that I will trust in You with all my heart.

I decree that as I submit my ways to You, You are making my path straight and leading me in the way I should go.

Psalm 32:8 says, *"I will instruct you and teach you in the way you should go; I will counsel you with my loving eye on you."*

I declare that Your counsel surrounds me. I decree that I will follow Your directions with courage, and I will wait with patience when You say, "Not yet."

Father, I declare that Your will is better than mine, Your timing is perfect, and Your direction is sure. I decree that my steps are ordered by the Lord, and I will walk in confidence, knowing You go before me. In Jesus' name, Amen.

Declaration:

I declare that I walk in divine wisdom and clarity. God directs my steps and orders my path. I will not be confused or afraid—God goes before me, and He leads me in peace.

Journal With Jesus

1. What decisions or situations do I need God's guidance in right now?

2. Have I truly invited God into this decision, or just asked Him to bless what I already want?

3. In which areas of my life should I pause and exercise patience, trusting in His impeccable timing?

Praying for Faith When Life Doesn't Make Sense

"Now faith is confidence in what we hope for and assurance about what we do not see.
—Hebrews 11:1, NIV

Sometimes prayer feels full of light and clarity.

And then there are the other times...

When the answers don't come.
When things fall apart instead of falling into place.
When all you have is a whisper of hope and the sound of your own tears.

That's when faith becomes more than a word. That is when you learn to pray with your eyes closed, not merely with your Bible open. It's not because you fully comprehend everything—rather, it's because you've made the conscious decision to trust regardless.

Faith Isn't Denial—It's Dependence

Having faith doesn't mean pretending everything's okay. It means saying:

"Lord, even if I don't understand this, I still believe You are good."

Faith is standing on God's promises even when your feelings are shaky. It involves choosing to speak the truth even when fear is overwhelming:

- "God, You are still with me."

- "You are still in control."

- "You are still working, even when I can't see it."

Job is one of the clearest examples of this kind of faith. He lost his health, his wealth, and even his children. Yet in the ashes, Job declared: *"Though he slay me, yet will I hope in him"* (Job 13:15). Faith didn't erase his grief, but it anchored him to God when life made no sense.

Faith Speaks When Feelings Falter

There will be days when your faith feels small. But Jesus said even mustard seed faith is enough to move mountains (Matthew 17:20).

So if all you can pray is: *"God, help me believe"*—that's enough.

God isn't moved by the size of your confidence; He's moved by the presence of your trust.

There have been many experiences when life didn't make sense at all. As a child, I struggled with abandonment and rejection. I couldn't understand why love felt distant or why home didn't feel safe. Later, as a young adult and single mother, I struggled too. I often wondered: *"God, where are You in this?"*

For a long time, I felt powerless and never thought I'd break free from pain and struggles. In those seasons, my prayers weren't long or eloquent. They were simple scriptures like Isaiah 40:31 and John 8:36.

I started declaring scriptures over my life and over areas where I felt bound.

Deliverance didn't always come instantly; my struggle didn't disappear overnight, but it came surely. The more I prayed scripture, the more I felt strongholds lose their grip.

Today, I stand as someone God has delivered from so much—and I believe He can do the same for anyone who calls on Him. Looking back now, I can see His hand—carrying me, providing for me, protecting me. Even when I didn't feel Him, He was there. That's what faith in the dark looks like.

Remember What He's Already Done

Sometimes the best way to have faith for what's ahead is to look back.

Psalm 77:11 says: *"I will remember the deeds of the Lord; yes, I will remember your miracles of long ago."*

Think of the times He carried you when you didn't even realize it. The doors that closed unexpectedly turned out to be shields of protection. He provided you with quiet ways in the wilderness.

Faith grows when we rehearse God's faithfulness.

Faith is like an anchor in a storm. You may still feel the waves, but the anchor keeps you from drifting away. Prayer in seasons that don't make sense is like throwing your anchor deep into God's Word, trusting He will hold you steady until the storm passes.

Hold On—Even When It Hurts

Faith doesn't make everything easy. But it makes you unshakable.

Your anchor is not in the problem or in the results, regardless of what life throws at you—sickness, loss, delay, or disappointment. It's in your God.

He is still good.
He is still able.
And He is still writing your story.

In Mark 4, when the disciples were caught in a storm, they cried out, *"Teacher, don't you care if we drown?"* (v. 38). Jesus calmed the wind and waves with a word. Their fear was real, but so was His power. The same Jesus who stilled storms then still speaks peace into our chaos today.

Prayer

Father, this season does not make sense to me. I do not understand what You are doing, but I declare that I trust who You are. Your Word says in Hebrews 11:1, *"Now faith is confidence in what we hope for and assurance about what we do not see."*

I decree that my faith is anchored in Your promises, even when my emotions fluctuate. I declare that my confidence is not in circumstances but in the God who never changes.

And it is written in 2 Corinthians 5:7, *"For we live by faith, not by sight."* Therefore, standing on your word, I declare that I walk by faith. I decree that I will not be shaken by what I see, because I trust in the unseen hand of God guiding my life.

According to Job 13:15, *"Though he slay me, yet will I hope in him,"* I decree that my hope remains steadfast in You, even when I don't understand Your ways.

I declare that my faith will endure because You are faithful.

Remind me, Lord, of what You have already done in my life. Let Your Word be my anchor when life feels shaky.

I decree that I will still pray, I will still trust, I will still believe, and I will live by faith until I see Your promises fulfilled. In Jesus' name, Amen.

Declaration:

I declare that my faith stands firm in every season. I walk by faith, not by sight. God is working all things for my good, and I trust Him—even in the unknown.

Journal With Jesus

1. Which parts of my life feel confusing or uncertain right now?

2. Where do I need to let go of my understanding and trust God's plan?

3. What are some testimonies of answered prayers that can help me believe for the future?

Praying for Healing: Body, Mind & Spirit

"He heals the brokenhearted and binds up their wounds." —Psalm 147:3, NIV

Healing is rarely just an event—it's a journey. And if you're walking through that journey today, here's the truth: **God sees you.**

He sees the pain in your body, the heaviness in your heart, and even the thoughts you've never said out loud. And He cares deeply. He is not distant from your pain; He is present in it.

He Is Still Jehovah Rapha—The God Who Heals

From the very beginning, God revealed Himself as **Jehovah Rapha**, "the Lord who heals." *"...for I am the Lord, who heals you."* (Exodus 15:26, NIV)

When Jesus walked this earth, He didn't only preach—He touched, restored, and healed.

The blind saw, the lame walked, and the brokenhearted were comforted.

And He has not changed.

Whether your pain is physical, emotional, or spiritual—you are never out of His reach.

Physical Healing

God cares about your body. He intricately formed your body in your mother's womb and is aware of every cell within it. When sickness, fatigue, or unexplained pain comes, you are invited to bring it to Him.

There was a time when I battled with physical exhaustion and emotional heaviness. The exhaustion left me battling migraines and body aches. Some nights, I prayed with tears just to have the strength to get through the next day. And while usually my body didn't change overnight, my spirit did. Hope replaced despair, and my faith grew stronger.

God met me—not always with instant healing, but with daily grace that carried me.

Your prayers matter, just like King Hezekiah's, who prayed for his life and was granted fifteen more years (2 Kings 20). You can pray:

"Lord, I believe You are my Healer. Touch my body. Restore what's been broken.

Strengthen me where I am weak. Bring health and wholeness in Jesus' name."

And as you take medicine, attend appointments, or wait on test results, know this: **healing isn't always instant, but it is always God's heart.**

There have been times when I prayed for a friend, a coworker, or a customer who asked for prayers, and God answered instantly; sometimes it took months, and they would return with a testimony, and I had even forgotten. However, there were also times when I prayed and nothing happened.

That didn't change the fact that God heals and that He is good all the time.

Isaiah 53:5 says, *"By His stripes we are healed."* Realize healing isn't just a possibility—it was already paid for on the cross. This truth should give you hope and courage to keep declaring healing over your life.

Emotional and Mental Healing

Some wounds don't show up on X-rays. They live in sleepless nights, quiet tears, and the anxious racing of your thoughts. But God sees those wounds, too.

Isaiah 26:3 promises: *"You will keep in perfect peace those whose minds are steadfast, because they trust in you."*

For a long time I carried unspoken grief from my childhood in Liberia—feeling abandoned, unseen, and alone by parents who should have cared and been there. Those memories followed me into adulthood, shaping how I viewed myself and how much I could trust others.

In my healing journey, I had to bring those hidden hurts to God in prayer so that true healing could begin.

Like the woman with the issue of blood who pressed through the crowd for her healing (Mark 5), we too must press into Jesus, believing that His presence can heal what no medicine can reach.

Pray:
"Lord, heal my mind and emotions. Uproot fear, lies, and shame. Replace them with your peace and truth. Renew my mind daily in You."

Spiritual Healing

Sometimes the deepest pain comes from feeling distant from God. Maybe unanswered prayers left you disappointed. Maybe you've wrestled with doubt, anger, or even shame.

Friend, hear me: God is not angry with you. He is reaching for you.

Joel 2:25 declares, *"I will repay you for the years the locusts have eaten..."* God restores wasted years, broken faith, and even shattered hope.

When I was rebuilding my life as a young single mom, I often felt spiritually drained. I questioned God's plan. But each time I opened my Bible and whispered a prayer, His Spirit reminded me, *"You are still mine. I can heal what you've lost."*

Return to Him. Healing begins not only in the body but also in the soul.

Keep Praying—Even While You Wait

Healing doesn't always come overnight. But every prayer, every whisper of Scripture, and every decision to choose faith over fear is part of your healing journey.

Every time you say, *"God, I trust You,"* you are walking in wholeness—even if the symptoms haven't changed yet.

Prayer

Lord, You are my Healer. You know every part of me—body, mind, and spirit. I bring before You the pain I've been carrying, the symptoms I've been fighting, and the silence I've been sitting in.

Your Word says in 1 Peter 2:24, *"He himself bore our sins in his body on the cross... and by his wounds you have been healed."*

I decree that I am healed by the stripes of Jesus. I declare healing over my body, mind, and spirit because of the cross.

Jeremiah 17:14 says, *"Heal me, Lord, and I will be healed; save me and I will be saved, for you are the one I praise."*

I decree that as I call on You, I am healed. I declare that You are the One who saves, restores, and makes me whole.

According to Psalm 107:20, *"He sent out his word and healed them; he rescued them from the grave."*

I decree that Your Word is alive and active in me, bringing healing to my body and rescue to my soul.

I declare that peace replaces anxiety, healing overtakes pain, and restoration comes to every place of loss.

Father, I trust You—not just for a moment of relief, but for a journey of wholeness. I decree that I walk in healing, I walk in peace, and I walk in strength through the power of Christ.

I believe I am healed. I believe I am restored. I believe I am saved from distress because Your Word is true and unshakable.

In Jesus' name, Amen.

Declaration:

*I declare that I am healed in Jesus'
name—physically, mentally, emotionally,
and spiritually. I receive God's restoring
power. Wholeness is my portion, and peace
is my inheritance.*

Journal With Jesus

1. What area of my life is most in need of
   healing right now?

2. Have I truly invited God into that place, or
   am I trying to carry it alone?

3. What would it look like to trust God daily
   for healing—even while I wait?

Praying for Your Family

Marriage, Children & Loved Ones

"But as for me and my household, we will serve the Lord." —Joshua 24:15, NIV

Prayer over your family is like building a roof. It may not stop the storm from coming, but it keeps those under the roof safe and dry.

Even when your house feels noisy, your children are struggling, or your marriage feels dry—every prayer you pray and every scripture spoken over your spouse or children adds another layer of covering.

It may not always feel powerful in the moment...

But in the unseen, God is working.

The seed of prayer you sow today will bear fruit in seasons when you're too overwhelmed to pray. There was a season in my life when my marriage was in disarray.

I was busy with the duties of a wife, occupied with a full-time job, caring for a toddler, managing schedules for two teenagers, and running a small business.

In that season I neglected prayer; spending time with God became "just another to do" on my list of many things. And all the busyness not only affected my mental health but also my marriage.

But, my friend, the grace of God is in every season of your life. While I could barely spend twenty minutes in the presence of God being still, the prayers I had prayed in the past bore fruit in that season.

God placed my name on the hearts of other believers; a mentor called me one very early morning. The Lord had woken her up and told her to pray for my marriage. She was unaware of my overwhelming feelings of depression and that I was ready to give up on my marriage, but God knew and disturbed her sleep for my benefit.

So, my friend, pray for your marriage; God saved mine, and He can save yours too. Never cease praying for your marriage and family.

Nehemiah's Prayer Wall

In the book of Nehemiah, the people of God rebuilt Jerusalem's broken wall. They worked with one hand on the stones and the other holding a sword (Nehemiah 4:17). Why? Rebuilding was not just about protection but also about identity, family, and faith.

Your prayers do the same thing. Every prayer you pray for your marriage or children is like placing another stone in the wall of their future. You may feel tired. You may not see the progress. But like Nehemiah, your persistence builds what the enemy cannot tear down.

Praying For Your Marriage

Marriage is more than companionship; it's a covenant. And covenants need covering.

Ecclesiastes 4:12 says, *"A cord of three strands is not quickly broken."* This is more than a poetic line—it's a reminder that God must be the third strand. Without Him, a marriage frays under pressure. With Him, it holds through storms.

When my husband and I first went to couples counseling, we were only three years into our marriage. One of the exercises our counselor suggested to us was praying together as a couple. Indeed, at first, it appeared quite uncomfortable, and to be honest, we only occasionally did it.

However, prayer did more than just assist us in coping—it strengthened our bond.

I've learned that when couples stop praying, they often start fighting against each other instead of for each other. And they experience decreased intimacy in the relationship, a lesser connection with prayer, and also a decrease in their relationship with God.

But the opposite happens when they start praying, especially praying together.

Praying For Your Children

Children are arrows in the hands of a warrior (Psalm 127:4). Arrows must be sharpened, aimed, and released. Prayer is how you do that.

Isaiah 54:13 promises: *"All your children will be taught by the Lord, and great will be their peace."*

I've seen this firsthand with my three sons—two teens and a toddler. Each stage comes with its battles: peer pressure, identity and personality struggles, and fears about the future. I cannot shield them from everything. But I can pray—and my prayers stretch further than my reach.

Like Hannah, who dedicated Samuel to the Lord (1 Samuel 1), we release our children into God's hands.

And His hands are stronger than ours could ever be.

Think of prayer like an umbrella in the rain. The umbrella doesn't stop the rain from falling, but it shields the ones under it.

When you pray for your marriage, your children, or loved ones, you're opening an umbrella of covering over them. They may still walk through storms, but they won't be drenched in despair. Your prayers hold back what would have swallowed them whole.

Praying for Loved Ones

Parents. Siblings. Friends. Neighbors. Even those who feel distant from God can find solace. Your prayers are not wasted.

James 5:16 reminds us: *"The prayer of a righteous person is powerful and effective."* You may not see change overnight. But every prayer is a seed planted. And God is faithful to water it.

Growing up in Liberia, my childhood home wasn't always a place of stability. Later, as a single mother raising my boys, I felt the weight of protecting them when I had so little strength. Prayer became my weapon.

I prayed when money was short, when fear was heavy, and when loneliness crept in.

Looking back, I see the fruit of those prayers—boys who are growing in wisdom and faith, not because I had all the answers, but because God honored my cries.

Prayer

My Lord, thank You for the precious gift of family. I lift my spouse, my children, and my loved ones before You. Build a wall of protection around us, and cover us like a shelter in the storm.

Your Word declares in Numbers 6:24–25, *"The Lord bless you and keep you; the Lord make his face shine on you and be gracious to you."*

I decree this blessing over my family. I declare that we are kept, we are covered, and we walk in the light of Your favor.

Lord, hold us together when life tries to pull us apart. Teach me to fight for my family in prayer, even when I feel weary. Isaiah 54:13 says, *"All your children will be taught by the Lord, and great will be their peace."* You teach my children, and I decree that peace prevails in every aspect of their lives.

I trust You to do what I cannot, Lord. I declare that Your plans for my family are greater than mine, and I surrender to Your will.

As for me and my household, I decree what Joshua 24:15 declares: *"But as for me and my household, we will serve the Lord."*

Cover us with Your love, surround us with Your mercy, and may our family serve You faithfully forever. In Jesus' name, Amen.

Declaration:

I declare that my family is blessed, protected, and guided by the Lord. We walk in unity, peace, and divine purpose. God's hand is on every member of my household.

Journal With Jesus

1. What "stones" do I need to rebuild in prayer for my family (trust, unity, protection)?

2. Who in my home or circle of loved ones most needs covering right now?

3. Where do I need to let God be the third strand in my relationships?

Praying for Peace in the Middle of Chaos

"You will keep in perfect peace those whose minds
are steadfast, because they trust in you."
—Isaiah 26:3, NIV

When Life Gets Loud

Peace doesn't mean the absence of noise. It means
the presence of God—right in the middle of it.

Jesus never promised, *"I'll give you peace when
everything calms down."* Instead, He said, "Peace
*I leave with you; my peace I give you. I do not
give to you as the world gives"* (John 14:27, NIV).

His peace is steady. It doesn't shift with your
paycheck, your schedule, or your surroundings.
His peace is strong enough to hold you even when
chaos is swirling.

In Mark 4:35–41, the disciples found themselves
in a violent storm. While they panicked, Jesus was
asleep in the boat. When they cried out for help,
Jesus came up; he rebuked the wind and waves,
and suddenly there was calm.

Here's the lesson: Peace isn't found in calmer circumstances—it's found in Christ's presence. The same Jesus who spoke to storms then still speaks peace into our storms today.

Think of prayer like noise-canceling headphones. The outside world doesn't stop making noise—the chaos is still there. But when you put the headphones that are prayers on, all of those disruptive sounds fade into the background. Prayer doesn't erase every problem, but it tunes your heart to God's frequency so you can hear His still, small voice above the noise.

Re-Centering in Prayer

When your thoughts are racing and your chest feels tight, peace comes from focus, not control.

That might look like:

- Whispering: *"Jesus, I trust You."*

- Meditating on a single verse like Philippians 4:6–7.

- Turning off the news and turning on worship.

- Resting when guilt says you should do more.

Peace doesn't come from fixing everything. It comes from surrendering everything.

As a mom, wife, and entrepreneur, I know chaos intimately. There was a season when I was balancing long hours at the bank, caring for my boys, and trying to launch my business. The pressure left me exhausted, short-tempered, and anxious. My prayers in that season weren't fancy—they were desperate.

Peace didn't come because my schedule lightened. It came because His presence strengthened me. That's the gift of prayer—it shifts the weight from our shoulders to His.

Speak Peace Into the Chaos

Proverbs 18:21 says, *"The tongue has the power of life and death."*

Your words create atmosphere. Don't just pray for peace—declare it:

- "I speak peace over this home."

- "I speak calm into my mind."

- "God's presence is greater than this pressure."

Prayer

My Lord and King, I am tired of carrying the chaos on my own. But Your Word says in John 14:27, *"Peace I leave with you; my peace I give you... Do not let your hearts be troubled and do not be afraid."*

I declare that Your peace rests on me now. I decree that fear and trouble cannot rule my heart, for Jesus has given me His peace.

Lord, I invite that peace to quiet my heart and my home. I speak peace over my family, my mind, and my day. Help me let go of what I cannot control, and teach me to trust that You are bigger than every difficulty I face.

I affirm Isaiah 26:3, *"You will keep in perfect peace those whose minds are steadfast because they trust in you."*

I declare that my mind is fixed on You. I decree that perfect peace surrounds me, flooding every part of my life and holding me steady when the storms come.

Your Word says in Psalm 29:11, *"The Lord gives strength to his people; the Lord blesses his people with peace."*

I declare this blessing over me and my family. I decree that Your peace will guard our hearts, strengthen our spirits, and cover us in every season.

Thank You, Father, that Your peace goes deeper than my understanding and carries me through hard times. In Jesus' name, Amen.

Declaration:

I declare that I walk in peace, not panic. God is with me in every storm. His peace guards my heart and mind, and no chaos can shake my foundation in Him.

Journal With Jesus

1. What areas in my life feel the most chaotic right now?

2. What am I trying to control instead of surrendering to God?

3. How can I begin declaring peace with my words this week?

Praying for Provision: Trusting God to Meet Every Need

"And my God will meet all your needs according to the riches of his glory in Christ Jesus."
—Philippians 4:19, NIV

God Knows Your Needs

Provision isn't only about money. It's about knowing—deep down—that you are cared for.

God sees the stack of bills, the empty fridge, the tuition deadlines, the job uncertainty, and the hidden fears you've whispered in prayer. And still, He declares, *"I will provide."*

Let me tell you, there was a season when I didn't know how I'd pay for rent or childcare as a single mom. I worked hard, but it never felt like enough. I cried out to God and prayed with my mouth, but I honestly doubted in my heart. I could not see a light at the end of the tunnel.

Yes, I read scriptures like Philippians 4:19: *"And my God will meet all your needs according to the riches of his glory in Christ Jesus."*

But during those times I had to pair that with Hebrews 11:16; my faith had to align with the written word in Philippians 4:19. I was praying the words but not believing them. I allowed the situations to speak louder.

And when that realization hit me, I had to repent and confess and started taking small steps of faith, writing down my request but also declaring the scriptures and believing. Declaring scriptures like Mark 11:24 and choosing to thank God in advance.

Miraculously, unexpected opportunities would open up, and needs were always met. That season taught me that God is truly Jehovah Jireh, my Provider.

He isn't just your Creator; He truly is **Jehovah Jireh**, the Lord who provides (Genesis 22:14).

When Abraham took Isaac up the mountain in Genesis 22, he had no idea how God would provide. Yet when Isaac asked, "Where is the lamb?" Abraham replied with faith, *"God himself will provide the lamb."* And He did—a ram caught in the thicket.

Here's the lesson: **God provides what we cannot see on the way up the mountain.** Provision often comes at the last possible moment, not because He's late but because He's teaching us to trust.

Provision Comes in Many Forms

Sometimes it's manna in the wilderness *(Exodus 16).*
Sometimes it's oil that doesn't run out *(1 Kings 17:16).*
Sometimes it's wisdom to stretch what you already have.

Provision is not always "more." Sometimes it's clarity, contentment, or peace in the waiting.

Think of provision like a child's lunchbox. A parent doesn't give a year's worth of food in one day. Instead, they provide what the child needs daily. Jesus said, *"Give us today our daily bread"* (Matthew 6:11).

God's provision is daily, not distant. He gives us enough for today so our trust stays in Him—not in the stockpile.

You Can Trust Him With the Practical

God isn't too holy to care about groceries, gas money, or overdue bills. He provides in both extraordinary and ordinary ways.

Sometimes He answers with abundance; other times He gives just enough for today so that we lean on Him again tomorrow.

Prayer

Father, thank You that You know every need I have, even the ones I don't speak out loud. Your Word says in Philippians 4:19, *"And my God will meet all your needs according to the riches of his glory in Christ Jesus."*

I declare today that You are my faithful Provider, and I trust You to meet every need in my life.

It is written in Psalm 23:1, *"The Lord is my shepherd; I lack nothing."*

I decree that I will not live in fear of lack, because You are my Shepherd who leads me, guides me, and makes sure I have everything I need.

You also said in Matthew 6:31–32, *"So do not worry, saying, 'What shall we eat?' or 'What shall we drink?'... Your heavenly Father knows that you need them."* Lord, forgive me for the times I've worried instead of trusting You.

Today I choose to let go of anxiety and fear, and I declare that my life is in the hands of a Father who knows and cares for me.

Stretch what I already have, Lord, and open my eyes to see Your abundance all around me.

Thank you for being my provider—not just today, but every day to come. I decree that my trust will remain in You, and I will testify of Your goodness.

In Jesus' name, Amen.

Declaration:

I declare that God is my provider. I lack no good thing. Every need is met, every debt is canceled, and every blessing is released in Jesus' name. I live in divine provision and overflow.

Journal With Jesus

1. What needs have I been trying to carry on my own?

2. Am I trusting more in my paycheck, savings, or abilities—or in God's ability to provide?

3. What are three ways God has provided for me in the past that I can remember and thank Him for today?

Praying for Courage in New Seasons

"Have I not commanded you? Be strong and courageous. Do not be afraid; do not be discouraged, for the Lord your God will be with you wherever you go." —Joshua 1:9, NIV

New Seasons Bring New Stretching

Every new season carries both excitement and fear. Starting a new job, stepping into ministry, becoming a parent, or moving into a new place—each requires courage. And courage is not the absence of fear, but the decision to move forward despite it.

Joshua faced one of the greatest transitions in Scripture—leading Israel after Moses' death. He likely felt overwhelmed and unqualified. Yet God's repeated command to him wasn't "be talented" or "be confident." It was, *Be strong and courageous... for the Lord your God will be with you"* (Joshua 1:9).

This shows us that courage is not about who we are—it's about who goes with us. God's presence is the foundation of our bravery.

Esther's story reminds us that courage may require risk. Facing possible death, she declared, "*If I perish, I perish*" (Esther 4:16). However, her obedience paved the way for deliverance.

Sometimes courage doesn't feel safe—but it is always secure when it rests in God's hands.

Think of stepping into a new season like crossing a bridge covered in fog. You can't see what's on the other side. But as you walk, you feel the bridge under your feet, and you know you are secure.

In the same way, God's promises are like that also; they support every step, even when you're not sure what will happen next.

A child who is learning to ride a bike might wobble and be afraid of falling. But the training wheels keep them steady. God's presence works the same way.

New seasons might feel uncertain, yet the hand of God keeps us balanced until we grow in confidence.

Gideon thought he was too weak, too little, and not good enough when God called him. But the angel said, "The Lord is with you, strong warrior" (Judges 6:12). Gideon wasn't brave because of his credentials; he was brave because God told him to be—it came from God's reassurance.

New seasons may show us where we fall short, but that's when God's strength shines the most.

Don't Wait to Feel Ready

Obedience usually comes before courage, not after. Peter didn't feel ready when he stepped out of the boat in Matthew 14. But the moment he moved in faith, he experienced the power of God holding him up.

You don't need to have all the answers. You just need to say, *"Yes, Lord."*

Prayer

Lord, I thank You for the new season You are leading me into. Even though I feel unsure, I declare that I am not alone—because it is written in Joshua 1:9, *"Have I not commanded you? Be strong and courageous. Do not be afraid… for the Lord your God will be with you wherever you go."* I decree that I will walk in strength and courage, not fear, because You are with me.

According to Isaiah 43:19, *"See, I am doing a new thing! Now it springs up; do you not perceive it?"* Father, I declare that You are already making a way for me. I may not see the full picture, but I decree that You are opening doors, clearing paths, and preparing the way ahead of me.

As it is written in 2 Timothy 1:7, *"For God has not given us a spirit of fear, but of power and of love and of a sound mind."*

I decree that fear will not control me. I declare that I walk in the power of Your Spirit, rooted in love, and steady in a sound mind.

Today, I choose faith over fear. I declare that my answer is "yes" to whatever You are calling me to, knowing You are already ahead of me. Thank You for being my strength, my courage, and my guide.

In Jesus' name, Amen.

Declaration:

I declare that I am bold and courageous. I am not afraid of change. I step into new seasons with faith, knowing that God is leading me to a purpose and breakthrough.

Journal With Jesus

1. What new season am I stepping into right now that feels overwhelming?

2. Which biblical example of courage (Joshua, Esther, Gideon, or Peter) speaks most to my situation?

3. What small step of obedience can I take today to show trust in God's presence?

Praying for Patience in the Waiting

"Wait for the Lord; be strong and take heart and wait for the Lord." —Psalm 27:14, NIV

The Weight of Waiting

Waiting is almost never comfortable. You've prayed, had faith, and done all you know to do, yet the doors remain closed and the answers don't seem to be in sight. It may feel like there is no light at the end of this very long tunnel.

But the truth is, waiting is not a waste of time. In God's kingdom, waiting seasons are working seasons.

When the Israelites left Egypt, the journey to the Promised Land could have been short. Instead, God led them through forty years in the wilderness (Deuteronomy 8:2). Why? This was done to humble them, test them, and prepare them for what lay ahead.

The waiting period wasn't to punish them—it was for preparation. The land was ready, but the people's minds needed reshaping.

The same is true for us today: God will often use delays to strengthen our faith and refine our character, not to punish us, because he loves us.

"Not only so, but we also glory in our sufferings because we know that suffering produces perseverance, perseverance character, and character hope. And hope does not put us to shame, because God's love has been poured out into our hearts through the Holy Spirit, who has been given to us." -Romans 5:3-5

In Luke 2, Simeon and Anna waited their entire lives to see the Messiah. They prayed, fasted, and served in the temple for decades. And when the day finally came, their eyes beheld God's promise fulfilled.

Their story teaches us that waiting in faith is never in vain—because God always keeps His word.

Think of a seed buried underground. For weeks, nothing appears on the surface. But in a hidden place, roots are forming and growth is happening. Just because you can't see progress doesn't mean nothing is happening. God often does His deepest work beneath the surface.

Waiting on God is like sitting at a red light. You're eager to move, but the signal hasn't changed. If you rush ahead, you risk collision.

However, if you wait, the green light appears precisely when you need it, guaranteeing your safety. God's timing isn't just about delay—it's about protection.

Isaiah 64:4 says: *"Since ancient times no one has heard, no ear has perceived, no eye has seen any God besides you, who acts on behalf of those who wait for him."*

Waiting is not inactivity—it is expectation. It is trusting that God is acting even when we cannot see it.

Active Patience

Patience doesn't mean doing nothing. It means doing what you can while trusting God with what you can't.

- Keep showing up in prayer.

- Keep speaking life over your situation.

- Keep leaning into His Word.

- Keep surrendering the timeline back to Him.

Psalm 130:5 reminds us, *"I wait for the Lord, my whole being waits, and in his word I put my hope."*

Microwaves are quick, but they can be shallow. Sometimes the microwave can heat the outside without affecting the inside. Ovens take longer, but they make food that is soft and properly cooked.

In the same way, God's process during waiting seasons may take longer, yet it leads to deeper and more significant change.

Prayer

Heavenly Father, waiting is not easy for me. Yet Your Word says in Romans 8:25, *"But if we hope for what we do not yet have, we wait for it patiently."* I declare that I will wait with hope, and I decree that patience will rise up in me as I trust in Your promises.

It is written in Lamentations 3:25–26, *"The Lord is good to those whose hope is in him, to the one who seeks him; it is good to wait quietly for the salvation of the Lord."* I declare that waiting is not punishment but preparation, and I decree that I will see Your goodness even in the waiting.

Psalm 27:14 says, "Wait *for the Lord; be strong and take heart and wait for the Lord."* I decree that my strength comes from You. I declare that I will be strong, take heart, and wait on You with steadfast faith.

Father, I surrender my timeline to You. I declare that Your plans for me are good and that Your timing is perfect. In Jesus' name, Amen.

Declaration:

I declare that my waiting is not wasted. God is working in the silence and shaping me in the stillness. I wait with hope, walk in trust, and worship while I wait.

Journal With Jesus

1. What prayer am I still waiting on God to answer?

2. Where can I recognize signs of God's unseen work, even if small?

3. Which biblical story of waiting (Israel, Simeon, and Anna) encourages me most today?

Praying for a Renewed Mind

"Do not conform to the pattern of this world, but be transformed by the renewing of your mind."
—Romans 12:2, NIV

Have you ever felt like your thoughts were your own worst enemy? The battlefield of prayer often begins in the mind. The good news is you don't have to stay stuck in toxic thinking. God offers us renewal, one thought at a time.

The Real Battlefield

The greatest battles are often invisible. They happen in our thoughts, in our self-talk, in the quiet moments when no one else can see the war—but God does.

The enemy knows if he can control your mind, he can control your peace. That's why renewing your mind isn't just positive thinking; it's spiritual warfare.

2 Corinthians 10:5 says, "...we *take captive every thought to make it obedient to Christ.*"

Paul uses the language of warfare here—*take captive.*

That means you don't let destructive thoughts roam free. You arrest them, confront them with Scripture, and replace them with truth.

Just as Jesus resisted Satan's lies in the wilderness by speaking Scripture (Matthew 4), we too are called to use God's Word as a weapon.

Think of your mind like a garden. If you leave it unattended, weeds (negative thoughts, lies, and fears) will grow quickly. But when you actively plant seeds of truth, water them through prayer, and uproot lies, the garden begins to flourish. A renewed mind is not automatic—it's cultivated.

Romans 12:2 doesn't just say, "Try harder to think better." It says, *"Be transformed."* This is the work of the Holy Spirit.

Transformation happens as we continually expose ourselves to God's Word. The Greek word for "transformed" here is *metamorphoo*—the same root as metamorphosis, like a caterpillar becoming a butterfly.

Renewal doesn't just improve your thinking; it changes your entire being from the inside out.

Imagine pouring dirty water through a filter. Slowly, the impurities are removed until clean water flows. God's Word works the same way in our minds—it filters out lies, shame, and fear, leaving clarity, peace, and truth.

You don't have to let your thoughts bully you. Replace every lie with truth:

- **Lie:** "I'm not good enough."
  Truth: "I am God's workmanship."
  (Ephesians 2:10)

- **Lie:** "Things will never change."
  Truth: "With God all things are possible."
  (Matthew 19:26)

- **Lie:** "It's too late for me."
  Truth: "God makes all things new."
  (Revelation 21:5)

Every time you replace a lie with truth, your mind is being renewed.

Here is a great analogy that I've heard: Imagine your mind as a radio. The enemy tries to fill the airwaves with static—fear, doubt, insecurity. But when you tune to the right frequency, you hear the clear signal of God's Word. Renewing your mind is like re-tuning your heart to God's channel every day.

So, my friend, there is hope, and that hope is found in turning to God's frequency. And that is wonderful news for me and you.

Start Small

Renewal doesn't happen overnight; it's a process, not an instant download.

Romans 12:2 reminds us:

"Do not conform to the pattern of this world, but be transformed by the renewing of your mind. Then you will be able to test and approve what God's will is—His good, pleasing, and perfect will."

Notice it says *"renewing"*—that's continuous. It's something we walk out daily.

I too struggle with negative, condemning thoughts, some days more than others, no matter how much I pray. But I've learned a few strategies through counseling that I want to share with you that will help you greatly.

Begin with one thought, one verse, and one prayer at a time

Here is how I learned to do this, from one of my counselors.

You don't have to overcome every negative belief in a single day.

Begin with one recurring thought that does not align with God's Word. Bring it into the light, identify it for what it is, and confront it.

- **One Verse at a Time:**

Find one scripture that speaks directly against that lie. For example, if the lie is *"I'm not good enough,"* replace it with *"I am fearfully and wonderfully made" (Psalm 139:14)*. Write it down. Put it on your mirror. Save it as your phone background. Let the Word saturate your mind until it becomes louder than the lie.

- **One Prayer at a Time:**

Don't underestimate the power of a simple prayer rooted in scripture. You can pray, *"Lord, I reject the lie that I am unworthy. Your Word declares that I am chosen, holy, and dearly loved (Colossians 3:12). I align my mind with Your truth today."*

This is how strongholds are dismantled—bit by bit, verse by verse, prayer by prayer. And yes, it works.

Another strategy I learned that has worked miraculously:

- **Rephrasing the lie:**

If the enemy whispers, *"You'll never overcome this,"* flip it immediately and declare, *"I can do all things through Christ who strengthens me"* (Philippians 4:13).

- **Cast it down completely:**

2 Corinthians 10:5 says, *"We demolish arguments and every pretension that sets itself up against the knowledge of God, and we take captive every thought to make it obedient to Christ."* The moment a toxic thought surfaces, refuse to entertain it. Replace it with truth.

I'll also suggest the use of **positive scripture-led affirmations.** Write these affirmations down on an index card or sticky notes.

Place the scriptures and affirmations on your desk, tape them to your mirror, put them on the back of your door, set them as your phone's screen saver, and speak them daily—morning and night.

Speak affirmations like these:

I have the mind of Christ: *"But we have the mind of Christ." —1 Corinthians 2:16*

I think on what is true, noble, right, pure, lovely, and praiseworthy. *"Whatever is true, whatever is noble, whatever is right, whatever is pure, whatever is lovely, whatever is admirable, if anything is excellent or praiseworthy—think about such things." —Philippians 4:8*

I am transformed by the renewing of my mind, and I walk in God's perfect will. *"Do not conform to the pattern of this world, but be transformed by the renewing of your mind." —Romans 12:2*

I take every thought captive and make it obedient to Christ: *"We take captive every thought to make it obedient to Christ." —2 Corinthians 10:5*

The peace of God guards my heart and my mind in Christ Jesus: *"And the peace of God, which transcends all understanding, will guard your hearts and your minds in Christ Jesus." — Philippians 4:7*

I set my mind on things above, not on earthly things: *"Set your minds on things above, not on earthly things." —Colossians 3:2*

I am not ruled by fear but by power, love, and a sound mind: "For God has not given us a spirit of fear but of power, love, and a sound mind." *—2 Timothy 1:7*

Renewing the Mind Takes Practice

Over time, these truths will begin to **rewire your thinking, reshape your mental patterns, and strengthen your faith.** The more you practice scripture-led affirmations, the more your mind aligns with the mind of Christ (1 Corinthians 2:16). And when your thoughts change, your emotions follow—and peace becomes the natural fruit.

But remember, renewing your mind is not a one-time event. It's not a switch that you flip, and suddenly every negative thought disappears. It's a **daily practice, a spiritual discipline, and a journey of grace.**

Be patient with yourself. If you've spent years believing lies, it will take consistent truth to reframe them. Think of it like strengthening a muscle: no one goes to the gym once and expects instant transformation. In the same way, your brain—the patterns of thought you've lived with for years—needs time to be retrained by God's Word.

Every time you take a lie and replace it with scripture, you are exercising that "faith muscle." And just like exercise, what feels difficult at first becomes easier with consistency. Romans 12:2 says, *"Be transformed by the renewing of your mind."* That transformation is ongoing—it's something God is doing in you as you partner with His Word.

So keep practicing. Keep affirming His promises. Keep speaking truth over yourself. Over time, your mind will be renewed, your thoughts will come into alignment with Christ, and your life will reflect the victory that's already yours in Jesus' name.

Prayer

Lord, You see every thought that runs through my mind—both the ones I speak out loud and the ones I try to hide. I declare that I am being transformed, as Romans 12:2 says, *"Do not conform to the pattern of this world, but be transformed by the renewing of your mind."* I decree that my mind is renewed by Your Spirit, not shaped by the world.

As it is written in 2 Corinthians 10:5, *"We take captive every thought to make it obedient to Christ,"* I decree that every lie is exposed and brought under the authority of Jesus. I declare that my thoughts are aligned with truth, not deception, and I decree that fear and defeat have no place in my mind.

Your Word says in Ephesians 4:23 that I am *"to be made new in the attitude of [my] mind."* Father, I declare that my thoughts are filtered by Your Word until peace and clarity remain. I decree that my mind is being renewed day by day, and I walk in the victory of Christ.

Thank You, Lord, that I do not have to live in fear or defeat. I declare that my mind belongs to You, and I decree that I will think with clarity, truth, and peace through the power of Your Spirit.

In Jesus' name, Amen.

Declaration:

I declare that I have the mind of Christ. My thoughts are clear, focused, and full of peace. Every lie is broken, and every truth is planted deep within me. My mind is renewed and transformed by God's Word.

Journal With Jesus

1. What lies have I been believing that don't align with God's Word?

2. What Scriptures can I begin to pray over my thoughts daily?

3. How can I intentionally "tend the garden" of my mind this week?

Praying for Justice: Standing in the Gap for Others

"Learn to do right; seek justice. Defend the oppressed. Take up the cause of the fatherless; plead the case of the widow." —Isaiah 1:17, NIV

Justice Is God's Heart

There are certain issues in this world that should deeply concern us, as they also grieve God's heart:

- Children without safe homes

- Single mothers stretched beyond their strength

- The innocent harmed by violence

- The voiceless ignored by systems

- Families structure breaking apart

When we pray for justice, we're not being political. We're being biblical. Psalm 89:14 declares,

"Righteousness and justice are the foundation of your throne."

God's throne rests on justice—meaning every prayer for justice aligns with His character.

In Ezekiel 22:30, God said: *"I looked for someone among them who would build up the wall and stand before me in the gap on behalf of the land…"*

To "stand in the gap" means intercession—praying for others where their own strength or voice feels absent. This is what Moses did when he interceded for Israel after their sin (Exodus 32:11–14). God was ready to judge, but Moses' prayer became a bridge of mercy.

When you pray for the oppressed, you become that bridge. Your voice rises in the gap, echoing God's own heart.

Picture a fence with a hole in it. Through the gap, danger can easily slip in. But if someone stands there—shielding, watching, interceding—those behind the fence remain safe.

In the same way, your prayers fill the gaps where others are vulnerable, shielding them with God's covering.

In Luke 18, Jesus told the story of a widow who continually sought justice from an unjust judge.

Though the judge didn't fear God or care about people, he eventually granted her request because of her persistence.

Jesus' point was clear: if even an unjust judge responds to persistence, how much more will a righteous God answer the cries of His people? Persistent prayers for justice shake heaven and move history.

Imagine prayer as a courtroom. The enemy stands as an accuser, pointing out faults. But when you intercede, you step up as an advocate—like a defense attorney pleading a case. And Jesus, our ultimate Advocate (1 John 2:1), joins His voice with yours before the Father. Justice is released not because we are worthy, but because He is.

Romans 8:26 reminds us: *"The Spirit himself intercedes for us through wordless groans."* Even tears, sighs, and silent grief become prayers when offered to God. Don't underestimate them. Heaven hears what your mouth can't form.

Prayer is like holding up a torch in a dark place. Darkness may still be present, but light pushes it back. Every prayer for justice pushes against the shadows, declaring that God's kingdom will break in where injustice once reigned.

Let Prayer Lead to Action

Justice prayers often stir justice actions. For Nehemiah, prayer over Jerusalem's broken walls led to rebuilding (Nehemiah 1–2). For you, it may look like giving, mentoring, advocating, or serving. Prayer is never wasted—it often becomes the spark that fuels action.

Prayer

My Lord, I lift up to You the oppressed, the overlooked, and the mistreated. Your Word says in Amos 5:24, *"Let justice roll on like a river, righteousness like a never-failing stream!"* I declare that Your justice will flow unhindered in homes, in communities, and in nations. I decree that righteousness will rise up and break through every place of darkness.

I declare Psalm 103:6, which says, *"The Lord works righteousness and justice for all the oppressed."* I stand by that word and decree that You are moving on behalf of the vulnerable. I decree that Heaven hears the cries of the overlooked and that You, Lord, are their Defender.

According to Micah 6:8, *"He has shown you… what is good. And what does the Lord require of you? To act justly and to love mercy and to walk humbly with your God."* I decree that my life, my words, and my prayers align with Your heart for justice and mercy.

I declare that I will stand in the gap—not in fear, but with bold faith—trusting that my prayers are a shield and my obedience is a light in dark places.

Father, let my intercession echo Your heart and become a vessel of Your fairness and mercy in the earth. I decree that justice, righteousness, and mercy will prevail, for You are a righteous Judge.

Jehovah Nissi, I pray for brothers and sisters all over the world who have to worship You in secret, preach the gospel even when it puts them in danger, and suffer just because they believe in Your name. Father, give them strength, and please surround them with angels to be their shields and a place to hide.

For every missionary who goes to a dangerous country... For every believer who is in jail because of their faith... For every oppressed Christian who is afraid but still has hope...

I am standing in the gap right now. Let them find peace in your presence. Let Your Word be their sword. Let your justice flow like water.

I cry out for them, trusting that You see, know, and will save them. I thank you for miracles in every area of their lives. In the powerful name of Jesus, Amen.

Declaration:

I declare that God is my Defender and my Deliverer. Justice is being released in every area of my life. No weapon formed against me will prosper, and no lie will stand. Righteousness will prevail.

Journal With Jesus

1. Who in my community or circle would most benefit from my support at this time?

2. What injustice weighs on my heart—and how can I pray persistently about it?

3. Is God calling me to act on behalf of the oppressed beyond prayer?

Praying for Purpose: Discovering Why You're Here

"For we are God's handiwork, created in Christ Jesus to do good works, which God prepared in advance for us to do." —Ephesians 2:10, NIV

The Ache For Purpose

There's a quiet ache in every heart: *"What am I here for?"*

We feel it in the monotony of daily routines.
We sense it when old dreams feel distant.
We wrestle with it when we've poured into others until we forget who we are.

But here's the truth: You were created on purpose, for a purpose, by a God who does not make mistakes.

Jeremiah 1:5 says, *"Before I formed you in the womb I knew you; before you were born I set you apart."*

God spoke this over Jeremiah before he had preached a single sermon. Purpose doesn't begin with what we achieve—it begins with God's design. The same is true for you. Before you ever took a breath, God already marked you with purpose.

Think of an architect's blueprint. Before the first brick is laid, the entire structure is already designed. In the same way, your life is not random—it follows a divine design. Even when you only see pieces, God sees the whole plan.

Ephesians 2:10 says, *"For we are God's handiwork, created in Christ Jesus to do good works, which God prepared in advance for us to do."*

That verse should assure you that you are not here by accident; you do have a purpose.

Purpose in the Ordinary

Sometimes we think "purpose" means platforms, titles, or applause. But in Scripture, God often used ordinary acts of faithfulness to accomplish extraordinary things.

- Ruth's loyalty to Naomi positioned her in the lineage of Christ.

- A boy's small lunch fed thousands in Jesus' hands (John 6).

- Dorcas's simple acts of sewing blessed her entire community (Acts 9:36–39).

Your purpose may look like encouraging a friend, raising your children in faith, serving quietly, or using your gifts in ways that no one else sees. The little things are not small for God.

When you buy a packet of seeds, you see the picture of what they'll become—a garden of flowers, a field of vegetables. But in your hand, they look insignificant. Purpose is like that.

You may not look like much now, but the potential God-given purpose that has been placed within you will grow into something greater when nurtured through obedience.

Romans 11:29 reminds us: *"For God's gifts and his call are irrevocable."*

Maybe you've wondered if you've missed your moment or if failure disqualified you. Scripture says otherwise. God doesn't revoke His calling. Seasons may shift, assignments may change, but His purpose for you remains intact.

A compass always points north, even if you turn it in every direction. Purpose is like that—it may take different shapes in different seasons, but it always points back to the same true north: loving God, loving people, and walking in obedience.

Keep Seeking, Keep Listening

Psalm 139:14 says: *"I praise you because I am fearfully and wonderfully made..."*

Purpose isn't something you invent; it's something you discover. Step by step, prayer by prayer, God unfolds the path He has already prepared.

Prayer

Father, there are moments when I wonder if my life truly matters, but Your Word reminds me that I was created with intention and for a purpose. It is written in Ephesians 2:10, *"For we are God's handiwork, created in Christ Jesus to do good works, which God prepared in advance for us to do."*

I declare that I am Your handiwork, designed with care, and I decree that my life carries divine purpose prepared by You.

It is written in Proverbs 19:21, *"Many are the plans in a person's heart, but it is the Lord's purpose that prevails."* I decree that no plan of mine, or of others, can override Your perfect purpose for me. I declare that my value is not found in status but in faithfulness to the call You've placed on my life.

According to Psalm 138:8, *"The Lord will fulfill his purpose for me."*

I decree that You will bring to completion the purpose You set for me before I was born. I declare that as I place my trust in You, I will see what you've put in my hands today, and I will use it with courage and faith.

Step by step, You are leading me into the good works You have already prepared. I decree that I will walk boldly in them, trusting that my life is aligned with Your plan. In Jesus' name, Amen.

Declaration:

I declare that I am chosen, called, and created for a divine purpose. I will walk boldly in God's assignment for my life. Every step I take is ordered, and nothing can stop the plan of God for me.

Journal With Jesus

1. What lies have I believed about my worth or purpose?

2. What gifts or strengths has God placed in me that I can begin using today?

3. What small step of obedience is God asking me to take in this season?

Praying for Humility: Staying Low Before the Lord

"Humble yourselves before the Lord, and he will lift you up." —James 4:10, NIV

Humility Isn't Weakness—It's Willingness

Willingness to say:

- *"God, I acknowledge that I don't have everything figured out, and that's okay."*

- *I'm going to stop striving and start trusting.*

- *I bow low so God can be lifted high.*

The world tells us, *"Promote yourself. Protect your image. Fight to be seen."*
But the kingdom calls us to a different posture: on our knees.

Philippians 2:6–8 tells us Jesus, though fully God, *"made himself nothing... he humbled himself by becoming obedient to death—even death on a cross.”*

If the Son of God chose humility as His path, how much more should we? True humility reflects Jesus, who exchanged heaven's throne for a manger and majesty for servanthood.

God Honors the Humble

Psalm 34:18: *"The Lord is close to the brokenhearted..."*
Isaiah 66:2: *"These are the ones I look on with favor: those who are humble and contrite in spirit..."*

God doesn't look for polish or perfection. He looks for hearts low enough to receive Him.

Imagine two cups—one full, one empty. A full cup cannot be filled. But an empty cup is ready to receive. Humility empties us of pride so God can fill us with His presence, wisdom, and grace.

Humility Isn't Self-Pity

It's not shrinking back or denying your worth. It's shifting your perspective:

- "Everything I have is a gift."

- "Everything I do is by grace."

- "I don't need to prove myself—I belong to the One who called me."

Humility is confidence rightly placed in God, not self.

In Luke 18:9–14, Jesus contrasts a Pharisee who boasted in prayer with a tax collector who simply cried, *"God, have mercy on me, a sinner."*

Jesus declared that the humble man went home justified. Why? Pride pushes God away, while humility invites His mercy.

Good soil must be broken to prepare the seeds to grow. Pride is like hardened ground that won't give in. Humility is like a soft soil that is ready to be planted with God's Word; it will produce fruit that lasts.

Pride Pushes; Humility Invites

- Pride says: *"I've got this."*

- Humility says: *"God, I need You."*

- Pride resists correction.

- Humility receives wisdom.

- Pride wants credit.

- Humility gives God glory.

Psalm 25:9 promises: *"He guides the humble in what is right and teaches them his way."*

A mirror reflects whatever is before it. Pride keeps the mirror pointed at ourselves. Humility turns the mirror toward God so He gets the glory.

Humility Keeps You Close to God

When your heart is humble, your prayers become honest. You stop performing and start depending.

The lower you go before Him, the higher His presence can lift you.

Be Aware of False Humility

There's a difference between true humility and false humility. True humility is not thinking less of yourself—it's thinking of yourself less and depending fully on God. But false humility looks spiritual on the outside while hiding fear and disobedience on the inside.

False humility whispers:

- *"I'm not qualified."*

- *"I don't know enough."*

- *"Surely God would choose someone else."*

At first, it sounds like modesty, but really, it's unbelief disguised as humility. It's saying, *"God, I don't believe You can use me."*

In 2021, God gave me the vision to write this very book. I wrote the initial manuscript, but I let it sit for almost five years. Why? Because I didn't think I was qualified. I told myself, *"I'm not a pastor. I'm not a prayer leader. I haven't even been saved long enough to write about prayer. Who am I to teach others?"*

So instead of moving forward in obedience, I stayed stuck in self-doubt. All the while, God had answered my prayers and given me powerful insight into the secret of praying His Word. But I disqualified myself.

One day while in prayer, I asked God to use me. Gently but firmly, the Holy Spirit reminded me, *"I've already given you an assignment, and you've left it undone."* At first, I didn't understand. I had done coaching and other projects. But when I prayed again, the conviction hit my heart—it was this book.

God had asked me to write it years before, and I had delayed in the name of "humility."

But the Holy Spirit corrected me: *"This isn't humility. This is disobedience. This is false humility."*

What the Bible Says

False humility isn't new. Moses wrestled with it at the burning bush. When God called him, Moses argued, *"Who am I that I should go to Pharaoh?"* (Exodus 3:11). Later he even said, *"Pardon your servant, Lord. Please send someone else"* (Exodus 4:13). What looked like humility was actually fear and unbelief.

The prophet Jeremiah said something similar: *"Alas, Sovereign Lord, I do not know how to speak; I am too young"* (Jeremiah 1:6). But God answered him: *"Do not say, 'I am too young.' You must go to everyone I send you to and say whatever I command you"* (Jeremiah 1:7).

In both cases, God didn't choose the "qualified." He chose the willing.

Remember, true humility says: *"God, I don't have it all together, but I trust You to work through me."* False humility says: *"God, I can't, and I won't."*

The truth is, none of us are "qualified" apart from Christ. But 2 Corinthians 3:5–6 reminds us: *"Not that we are competent in ourselves to claim anything for ourselves, but our competence comes from God. He has made us competent as ministers of a new covenant.*"

When we step out in obedience, God gets the glory. Our weakness becomes the very place His strength shines.

When I repented, pulled out my old laptop and pulled up the manuscript, I tell you, the Holy Spirit just poured like a stream; in three months I had written not only this book but three others. All did not come in my strength but in the strength and according to the will of God.

Prayer

Lord, I humble myself before You today. I lay down pride, my image, and my need to control. Your Word says in James 4:6, *"God opposes the proud but shows favor to the humble."*

I declare that I walk in Your favor as I choose humility. I decree that pride will not rule my heart, for I bow low before You.

James 4:10 says, *"Humble yourselves before the Lord, and he will lift you up."* I declare that when I choose humility, You will lift me in Your time and in Your way.

I decree that my life will reflect Your glory—not because of my strength, but because of Your grace.

According to Philippians 2:3, *"Do nothing out of selfish ambition or vain conceit. Rather, in humility value others above yourselves."* I decree that I will walk with a teachable spirit, valuing others above myself.

I declare that my words, my actions, and my attitude will be marked by humility and love.

Thank You, Father, for giving your grace. I decree that my heart will remain soft before you, and I revere you for who you are. In Jesus' name, Amen.

Declaration:

I declare that I walk in humility and grace. Pride has no place in me. I serve with love, lead with integrity, and follow Jesus with a humble heart.

Journal With Jesus

1. Are there areas where I've been trying to take control instead of trusting God?

2. How has pride shown up in my thinking, speaking, or reacting lately?

3. What does walking in humility look like in my relationships, prayers, and daily life?

Praying for Hope: Holding On in Hard Time

"Why, my soul, are you downcast? Why so disturbed within me? Put your hope in God, for I will yet praise him, my Savior and my God."
—Psalm 42:11, NIV

What do you do when life punches you in the gut, and prayer feels like the last thing you want to do? Hard times aren't meant to break us—they're meant to build us. And prayer is how we survive the storm.

Hope Isn't Just a Feeling

Hope is more than optimism or wishful thinking. In Scripture, hope is a firm foundation—an anchor that keeps you steady when the storms are strong.

Romans 15:13 says: *"May the God of hope fill you with all joy and peace as you trust in him..."* Hope doesn't come from circumstances. It comes from God Himself.

Romans 4:18 tells us Abraham, *"against all hope, in hope believed..."* Though his body was old and Sarah's womb barren, he held onto God's promise of a son. His hope wasn't in what he saw, but in the God who had spoken.

True hope doesn't deny the facts—it depends on the faithfulness of God.

Hebrews 6:19 calls hope *"an anchor for the soul, firm and secure."* Picture a ship on restless waters. The waves still crash, but the anchor holds it steady. That's what hope does—it doesn't remove the storm, but it keeps you from drifting away in despair.

Psalm 42 doesn't end in despair but in a declaration: *"...for I will yet praise Him."*

The word *"yet"* is powerful. It means:

- I haven't seen it yet—but I will praise.

- I don't feel it yet, but I will believe.

- I haven't received it yet, but I will wait in trust.

Hope thrives not because circumstances change, but because God never does.

Hope is like a single candle in a dark room. It may not light the whole house, but it pushes back the darkness enough for you to take the next step.

You don't need the whole plan—just enough light to keep moving forward.

In one of the darkest books of the Bible, Jeremiah still declares: *"Yet this I call to mind and therefore I have hope: Because of the Lord's great love we are not consumed, for his compassions never fail"* (Lamentations 3:21–22).

Hope is not the denial of pain—it's the decision to remember God's love in the middle of it.

When rock climbers lose their grip, the safety knot holds them. Hope works the same way. When your strength slips, hope in Christ keeps you tied to His promises. You may feel weak, but you are never bound to your situation; you have hope in Jesus.

Even Jesus Wept

Hope doesn't cancel grief. John 11 shows Jesus weeping at Lazarus's tomb even though he knew resurrection was coming. Hope allows us to feel pain while still believing that joy will have the final word.

An anchor only works when it sinks deep enough to reach the solid seabed. If it dangles in shallow water, the ship will drift. Hope works the same way—it can't rest in temporary fixes or human solutions. It must go deep into God's eternal promises. That's where the soul finds stability.

Prayer

Father God, when I am tired, remind me of Your faithfulness. Your Word says in Romans 15:13, *"May the God of hope fill you with all joy and peace as you trust in him, so that you may overflow with hope by the power of the Holy Spirit."*

I declare that my hope is not in results but in You, the God who never fails. I decree that joy, peace, and overflowing hope will rise up in me by the power of Your Spirit.

"I will yet praise him." I decree that even when I feel low, I will put my hope in You. -Psalm 42:5. I declare that I will lift my voice in praise, knowing that my soul finds strength and renewal in Your presence.

Isaiah 40:31 says, *"But those who hope in the Lord will renew their strength."* I declare that as I wait on You, my strength is renewed. I decree that I will wait with faith, pray with hope, and speak life even in hard seasons.

Thank You, Lord, that my hope is never wasted. I declare that You are still working, still moving, and still holding me securely in Your hands.

In Jesus' name, Amen.

Declaration:

I declare that hope is alive in me. My future is in God's hands. I will not give up—I will rise, I will believe, and I will hope again, because God is faithful.

Journal With Jesus

1. What situation has made it hard for me to hold on to hope?

2. What truth from Scripture can I anchor myself to when my emotions feel heavy?

3. What does it look like to say, *"I will yet praise You,"* in my life today?

Praying for Revival: A Fresh Outpouring of God's Spirit

"Will you not revive us again, that your people may rejoice in you?" —Psalm 85:6, NIV

For years, the church has been praying for revival. But realize that revival begins with you and me. Psalm 85:6 says, *"Will you not revive us again, that your people may rejoice in you?*

That verse should light a fire in your spirit.

Revival Doesn't Start in a Crowd—It Starts in a Heart

Revival isn't about a tent meeting, an emotional song, or a traveling preacher. True revival begins quietly in the secret place, when one heart grows hungry for more of God.

It is the rekindling of love, the reawakening of prayer, and the fire of the Spirit igniting dry bones.

When we pray for revival, we aren't asking for noise—we're asking for **holy fire.**

Think about a fireplace in winter. If you light it once and never tend to it, the flame eventually dies. Revival is like that fire; it requires ongoing tending. Logs must be added, ashes cleared, and oxygen given.

In the same way, our faith grows cold when neglected. But when we return daily to Scripture, prayer, worship, and repentance, we fan the flames of revival. God provides the spark, but we choose whether the fire will burn brightly or fade.

Revival Begins With Us

We often pray, *"Lord, change the world."* But revival whispers back, *"Lord, change me."*

2 Chronicles 7:14 is the foundation of revival:

> *"If my people, who are called by my name, will humble themselves, pray, seek my face, and turn away from their wicked ways, then I will hear from heaven, and I will forgive their sin and heal their land."*

Notice the order: revival begins with humility, repentance, and seeking His face. Before God heals a nation, He heals a heart.

Nehemiah saw the broken walls of Jerusalem and was overwhelmed with grief. But revival began not with bricks, but with ***prayer and repentance***. He confessed the sins of the nation, fasted, and cried out to God (Nehemiah 1:4–11).

Only then did God open the door for restoration. Nehemiah's story shows us that revival is always preceded by prayer and personal surrender.

Revival in Our Homes

You don't need a stadium. Revival can start around your kitchen table.

Pray, *Lord, let revival begin in my living room. Let my children hunger for Your Word. Let my home be filled with worship instead of worry.*

God, please stir my heart first—revive my prayer life, renew my passion, and reignite my love for your presence. And He will. Once your personal fire begins to burn, it will start to spread, encouraging those around you.

When even one mother, father, or young believer invites God's Spirit into their home, the atmosphere shifts. Like yeast in dough, the presence of God spreads until everything is transformed.

Don't Be Afraid to Ask for More

God never intended for us to live lukewarm, halfway lives. He created us to burn with holy passion.

Ask boldly:

- *"Lord, revive what's grown cold."*

- *"Set my heart ablaze again."*

- *"Use me as a spark for my family, my community, and my generation."*

Revival isn't something we watch happen—it's something we carry. And revival isn't just a corporate move; it starts with one surrendered heart.

Prayer

Father, I don't want to settle for routine faith. Your Word says in Psalm 85:6, *"Will you not revive us again, that your people may rejoice in you?"* I declare that revival begins in me. I decree that my heart, my home, and my generation will rejoice in You as You pour out Your Spirit.

As it is written in 2 Chronicles 7:14, *"If my people, who are called by my name, will humble themselves and pray... then I will hear from heaven..."* I decree that as I humble myself, seek Your face, and turn from distraction, Heaven responds. I declare that You are faithful to heal and restore.

I decree that I am awakened to Your presence. I declare that the fire of Your Spirit burns away apathy and reignites passion for You.

Let Your Spirit fall fresh on me, Lord, and let the flame spread to my family, my community, and my generation.

I decree that revival fire will not be contained but will overflow everywhere you send me. In Jesus' name, Amen.

Declaration:

I declare that revival begins in me. My heart is on fire for God. I will not grow weary or cold. I walk in power, hunger, and spiritual awakening.

Journal With Jesus

1. Where have I grown spiritually dry or distant without realizing it?

2. What would revival in my home look like?

3. What one bold prayer can I begin praying today for a fresh outpouring of the Holy Spirit?

Praying for Rest: Receiving God's Gift of Renewal

"Come to me, all you who are weary and burdened, and I will give you rest." —Matthew 11:28, NIV

Rest Is Obedience, Not Laziness

Let me be honest with you—I struggle with rest. As a wife, a mom of three, a full-time employee, and a woman running a small business while mentoring others, I often feel like there's no room to breathe. Even when my body slows down, my mind races with the next task, the next need, or the next crisis.

Maybe you feel the same way. Our culture glorifies hustle. It tells us that exhaustion is proof we're working hard enough. But God whispers something different: *"Come to Me."*

Rest isn't laziness—it's obedience. It means choosing to trust God more than we trust our to-do lists. Every time I resist rest, what I'm really saying is, *"It all depends on me."* But when I choose rest, I declare, *"God, my life depends on You."*

Carrying What God Never Asked You To

I've learned that many of my burdens aren't from God at all. They come from:

- Trying to meet everyone's expectations.

- Carrying endless to-do lists.

- Worrying about money, family, and the future.

Psalm 127:2 reminds us: *"In vain you rise early and stay up late, toiling for food to eat— for He grants sleep to those He loves."*

Friend, you are loved. You don't have to prove yourself by how much you produce. God gives rest as a gift, not as a reward you have to earn.

Rest Is Spiritual, Not Just Physical

I have experienced nights of eight hours of sleep and still awakened feeling exhausted—because my soul continued to bear burdens I never entrusted to God. That's why Jesus doesn't just promise rest for our bodies; He promises rest for our souls (Matthew 11:29).

Isaiah 40:29–31 says: *"He gives strength to the weary and increases the power of the weak… Those who hope in the Lord will renew their strength. They will soar on wings like eagles."*

This is the kind of rest that renews you inside and out, lifting you above chaos and reminding you that you were never meant to carry life alone.

Even God Rested

Think about it—even God, who never grows tired, rested on the seventh day (Genesis 2:2–3). He didn't rest because he needed to—he rested to show us we do need rest.

Sabbath is God's rhythm of love. It's His way of saying, *Stop. Breathe. Delight. Trust.*

Jesus in the Storm

One of my favorite pictures of rest is in Mark 4:37–39. The disciples were panicking in a storm, but where was Jesus? Asleep in the boat. When they woke Him, He spoke, *"Peace, be still."*

That challenges me. Jesus carried the calm of heaven into the chaos of earth. That's what resting in God does—it anchors us in storms so that we're not shaken by waves.

Permission to Pause

My dear friend, you don't have to earn rest. You just have to receive it. And I'm not preaching this at you; I'm also reminding myself. Here's something I learned about rest.

Rest may look like:

- Turning off your phone for an hour.

- Saying "no" without feeling guilty.

- Taking a walk and thanking God with every step.

- Or simply sitting in silence, breathing deeply in His presence.

These moments don't make you irresponsible; they make you available to God's renewal. Rest is not punishment; it is provision.

Here's what I want you to know: You're not alone if rest feels hard. I'm walking this journey too, learning to accept God's gift of renewal, one pause at a time.

And the same God who told Elijah to *"Get up and eat, for the journey is too much for you"* (1 Kings 19:7) is the same God telling you and me today:

"Rest. Be restored. Let me carry what you cannot."

Prayer

Dear Lord, Father, I confess that I have been running on empty, carrying burdens You never asked me to carry. But Your Word says in Matthew 11:28, *"Come to me, all you who are weary and burdened, and I will give you rest."*

I declare that I come to You, Lord, and I receive the gift of rest. I decree that weariness will no longer define me, for You are my strength and my renewal.

The scriptures say in Psalm 4:8, *"In peace I will lie down and sleep, for you alone, Lord, make me dwell in safety."* I declare that I will rest without fear. I decree that peace will guard my heart and my mind, and I will dwell securely because You watch over me.

According to your word in Exodus 33:14, *"My Presence will go with you, and I will give you rest."* I decree that I will not run ahead of You but walk in step with Your Presence. I declare that as I pause, You fill me with renewal in my body, mind, and spirit.

Today, I lay everything down at Your feet. I decree that I will pause without guilt, rest without fear, and trust You with what I cannot control. I receive Your peace and rest now, in Jesus' name. Amen.

Declaration:

I declare that I live in divine rest. I am not ruled by stress or fear. My soul finds rest in God alone. His peace surrounds me, and His grace sustains me.

Journal With Jesus

1. What burdens am I carrying that God never asked me to?

2. What practical step can I take this week to create space for soul rest?

3. How is God inviting me to trust Him by slowing down?

Praying for Joy: Delighting in God No Matter What

"The joy of the Lord is your strength."
—Nehemiah 8:10, NIV

There were times when joy felt out of reach, especially in seasons of stress and discouragement. I thought joy depended on circumstances, but then I discovered Psalm 16:11: *"You make known to me the path of life; you will fill me with joy in your presence."*

That verse shifted my perspective—joy wasn't something I had to chase; it was something I received in God's presence. Even in the middle of chaos, I could still have joy because it came from Him, not my situation. Today, I see joy as my strength (Nehemiah 8:10) and my inheritance as His daughter.

Joy Is Strength, Not Surface-Level

Joy isn't a fake smile or forced positivity. It is not about denying reality or pretending we're fine. Joy is a steady current beneath the surface of life—a holy strength that carries us when circumstances are heavy.

- Happiness depends on what happens.

- Joy depends on who holds us.

Paul described this in Philippians 4:13: *"I can do all this through him who gives me strength."* Joy is not an accessory to the Christian life—it is the very power that sustains us.

Jesus said, *"I am the vine; you are the branches. If you remain in me and I in you, you will bear much fruit"* (John 15:5).

Joy is like the fruit growing on the branch. You can't tape apples onto a lifeless stick and call it alive. In the same way, we can't manufacture joy. It only flows naturally when we remain connected to Christ.

Think of a branch cut off from a tree. At first, it looks alive, but within days it withers. Some of us live like that spiritually—disconnected; we try to fake fruit. But true joy requires abiding. Staying plugged in to His presence allows joy to flow effortlessly, just as sap flows through the vine into the branch.

Paul wrote Philippians—the "letter of joy"—while in chains. He declared: *"Rejoice in the Lord always. I will say it again: Rejoice!"* (Philippians 4:4).

Joy doesn't erase grief or cancel hardship. Instead, joy refuses to allow pain to have the final say. Joy says:

- "I may be grieving, but I'm still grateful."

- "I may be waiting, but I'm still worshiping."

- "I may not know the outcome, but I know my God."

Yes, there were many experienced seasons when I felt completely worn down. Balancing work, motherhood, and everything else left me drained. Financial struggles loomed, and prayers I had prayed for years felt unanswered. Yet I had to believe in the Scriptures: *"The joy of the Lord is your strength."*

It wasn't laughter at a joke or relief from my situation. It was a supernatural strength that rose up in me. The bills were still there, the struggles hadn't vanished, but I could breathe again. In those moments, I understood—joy does not depend on external circumstances; it resides within you.

God Sings Over You

Zephaniah 3:17 paints an incredible picture: *"The Lord your God is with you, the Mighty Warrior who saves. He will take great delight in you; in his love he will no longer rebuke you, but will rejoice over you with singing."*

Can you imagine? The Creator of the universe sings over you. Joy begins not with our songs to Him, but with His song over us.

The Joy Set Before Him

Hebrews 12:2 says Jesus endured the cross *"for the joy set before him."* That joy wasn't in the pain of crucifixion but in the victory that would come, our salvation.

This shows us that sometimes joy is found not in the present moment but in the hope of what God has promised.

Picture a balloon filled with helium. It rises, not because the weight disappears, but because what fills it is greater than what surrounds it.

Life's struggles may be like weights pulling down, but when filled with the Spirit, joy lifts us above what should crush us. Just as a balloon rises higher the more it's filled, our joy increases the more we're filled with God's presence.

Mary's Song of Joy

When the angel told Mary she would bear the Messiah, her life became more complicated, not less. Yet she sang: *"My soul glorifies the Lord and my spirit rejoices in God my Savior"* (Luke 1:46–47).

Mary's joy wasn't based on comfort but on calling. Joy is born in the presence of God, not in the absence of struggle.

Laughter Is Holy Too

Sometimes the most spiritual thing you can do is laugh with your kids, your spouse, or your friends.

- Laughter heals.

- Laughter restores.

- Laughter testifies that sorrow doesn't have the last say.

Proverbs 17:22 reminds us: *"A cheerful heart is good medicine, but a crushed spirit dries up the bones."* God designed joy to be healing for body, soul, and spirit.

Prayer

Lord, fill me with Your joy—the kind that does not fade but endures. Your Word says in Nehemiah 8:10, *"The joy of the Lord is your strength."*

I declare that Your joy strengthens me when I feel weak, and I decree that no circumstance will steal the joy that comes from You.

For it is written in Psalm 16:11, *"You make known to me the path of life; you will fill me with joy in your presence."* I declare that in Your presence, I am filled with joy.

I decree that my heart will laugh again and my soul will sing again, because joy flows from being near You.

1 Peter 1:8 declares, *"Though you have not seen him, you love him... you believe in him and are filled with an inexpressible and glorious joy."*

I decree that my faith fills me with a joy that cannot be explained and cannot be taken away. I declare that I receive this gift of joy today—not because everything is perfect, but because You are here with me, and Your presence is enough.

Let joy rise up in me like a river that no trial can dry up. I decree that I will delight in You no matter what. In Jesus' name, Amen.

Declaration:

I declare that the joy of the Lord is my strength. I live with joy, not sorrow. Joy is rising in my heart, filling my home, and overflowing into every part of my life.

Journal With Jesus

1. When was the last time I truly felt joy, and what helped me experience it?

2. What does it look like to choose joy even in the middle of hard things?

3. How can I begin to delight in God more fully in this season?

Section Three

A Heart Set on Prayer: Scripture-Led Prayer for Every Season of Life.

Acknowledgement

Dear Brother/Sister,

Thank you for journeying through these pages with me.

You've cried prayers of surrender, whispered words of hope, and lifted up your heart to a God who always listens. And now, as a gift for your quiet moments, this final section is here for you to keep praying.

Here, you'll find 25 prayer points rooted in God's Word and tailored for real-life struggles and seasons.

You can use this section:

- As part of your daily devotional

- To pray through specific situations

- When you don't know what to say, but you still want to pray

- Or to speak over your loved ones, your children, and even your community

These aren't fancy words.

Their hearts cry.

And they are heard by a God who is close, compassionate, and full of power.

After each prayer point, create a space for journaling with Jesus so you can process what God is stirring in your heart.

Take your time. You are welcome to return whenever you find it necessary.

This space is for you—to reset, refocus, and rest in prayer.

Let's begin with the first prayer:

A Prayer of Surrender—Letting Go of Control

"Trust in the Lord with all your heart and lean not on your own understanding; in all your ways submit to him, and he will make your paths straight." —Proverbs 3:5–6, NIV

Prayer:

Heavenly Father, I release my need to control every outcome. Your Word says that when I trust You with all my heart, You will direct my path. Today, I lay down my fears, my plans, and my expectations at Your feet. I declare Proverbs 3:5–6 over my life—my ways are submitted to You, and You are making my path straight. I choose faith over worry, surrender over striving, and obedience over self-reliance. Not my will, but Yours be done. In Jesus' name, Amen.

A Prayer for Healing—Physical, Emotional, and Spiritual Restoration

"He heals the brokenhearted and binds up their wounds." —Psalm 147:3, NIV

Prayer:

Jehovah Rapha, You are my healer. I declare Psalm 147:3—You heal the brokenhearted and bind their wounds. Father, I present every place in me that feels broken—my body, my emotions, and my spirit. By the stripes of Jesus, I am healed, according to your word in Isaiah 53:5. I receive restoration, strength, and peace. Anxiety must bow, pain must leave, and sorrow must be turned into joy. I trust that You are still the God who heals, and I receive my healing now. In Jesus' name, Amen.

A Prayer for Peace—Calm in the Middle of Anxiety, Chaos, or Storms

"You will keep in perfect peace those whose minds are steadfast, because they trust in you." —Isaiah 26:3, NIV

Prayer:

Prince of Peace, I thank You for Your promise in Isaiah 26:3 that You will keep me in perfect peace when my mind is fixed on You. Lord, I silence every anxious thought and declare John 14:27—Your peace, not the world's peace, rules in my heart. I speak, "Peace, be still," to every storm in my life. Fear has no place in me. Confusion must bow. I receive calm, clarity, and confidence through Christ Jesus. Lord, the world around me may be noisy, but I choose to quiet my heart in you. I place my trust in you, not in what I see, but in who you are. Thank you for being my shelter, my calm, and my safe place. I receive Your peace now. In Jesus' name, Amen.

A Prayer for Wisdom—Clarity to Make Right Decisions

"If any of you lacks wisdom, you should ask God, who gives generously to all without finding fault, and it will be given to you."
—James 1:5, NIV

Prayer:

Father, I ask according to James 1:5, and I believe You give wisdom generously to those who ask. Today, I declare that I will not lean on my own understanding but seek Your guidance in all things. Give me discernment to see beyond what is natural and recognize what is of Your Spirit. Help me choose paths that honor You. I resist confusion, and I receive clarity, insight, and divine understanding. My steps are ordered by the Lord according to Psalm 37:23, and I will walk in wisdom in Christ Jesus. Let me be guided not by fear or pressure, but by your Spirit. I'm listening, Lord—speak to my heart. In Jesus' name, Amen.

A Prayer for Provision—Financial Needs, Daily Bread, and Resources

"And my God will meet all your needs according to the riches of his glory in Christ Jesus." —Philippians 4:19, NIV

Prayer:

Jehovah Jireh, my Provider, I declare Philippians 4:19 over my life—You will supply all my needs according to Your riches in glory. You know every bill, every obligation, and every hidden concern, and I trust You to provide. As I seek first Your kingdom and righteousness, all these things are being added unto me as it is written in Matthew 6:33. Lack has no power over me. Worry has no hold on me. I receive provision, abundance, and overflow in Jesus' name. Amen.

A Prayer for Strength—Endurance Through Trials, Stress, or Weakness

"But those who hope in the Lord will renew their strength. They will soar on wings like eagles; they will run and not grow weary. they will walk and not be faint."
—Isaiah 40:31, NIV

Prayer:

Lord, I'm tired—in my body, in my mind, and deep in my soul. Sometimes it feels like too much. But I know that you're my strength. Lord, I declare Isaiah 40:31 over my life—my strength is being renewed as I place my hope in You. When I feel weak, I confess 2 Corinthians 12:10: *"When I am weak, then I am strong."* Father, fill me with endurance, stamina, and divine energy to run my race without growing weary. I refuse to faint, because the joy of the Lord is my strength, as written in Nehemiah 8:10. I rise today on the wings of an eagle. In Jesus' name, Amen.

A Prayer for Forgiveness. Releasing Guilt and Shame, Seeking God's Mercy

"If we confess our sins, he is faithful and just and will forgive us our sins and purify us from all unrighteousness." —1 John 1:9, NIV

Prayer:

Merciful Father, I confess my sins and declare 1 John 1:9—You are faithful and just to forgive me and cleanse me from all unrighteousness. By the blood of Jesus, guilt and shame have no power over me. Romans 8:1 says there is no condemnation for those in Christ Jesus, so I reject every lie of the enemy and receive Your grace. I forgive myself because You have forgiven me. I walk in mercy, freedom, and restoration. In Jesus' name, Amen.

A Prayer for Compassion. Softening the Heart Toward Others

"Be kind and compassionate to one another, forgiving each other, just as in Christ God forgave you." —Ephesians 4:32, NIV

Prayer:

Lord, I declare Ephesians 4:32 over my life—let kindness and compassion flow through me. Remove bitterness, hardness, and offense from my heart. Help me to see people through Your eyes. Colossians 3:12 says I am chosen, holy, and dearly loved, so I clothe myself with compassion, kindness, humility, gentleness, and patience. Let me love the unlovable and forgive quickly, just as You forgave me. In Jesus' name, Amen.

A Prayer for Protection—Safety from Harm, Danger, or Evil Influences

"The Lord will keep you from all harm—he will watch over your life; the Lord will watch over your coming and going both now and forevermore." —Psalm 121:7–8, NIV

Prayer:

Father, I decree Psalm 121:7–8—You are keeping me from harm and watching over my life. I declare Isaiah 54:17—no weapon formed against me or my household shall prosper. I plead the blood of Jesus over my home, my family, and everything connected to me. I release Psalm 91 over us—angels are guarding us, no plague shall come near our dwelling, and we are covered under the shadow of the Almighty. I declare, You are my shield, my refuge, and my defender. In Jesus' name, Amen.

A Prayer for Guidance—Direction in Life Choices and Purpose

"Whether you turn to the right or to the left, your ears will hear a voice behind you, saying, 'This is the way; walk in it.'" —Isaiah 30:21, NIV

Prayer:

Sometimes, Lord, I find myself uncertain about the path to take. The path ahead feels unclear, and I would rather not move without you. Lord, I declare Isaiah 30:21—I hear Your voice saying, "This is the way, walk in it." I refuse confusion and declare Proverbs 3:6—in all my ways I acknowledge You, and You direct my path. Guide me with peace, confirm me with wisdom, and order my steps according to Psalm 37:23. I will not be led by fear or pressure but by the Spirit of God. Your Word is a lamp to my feet and a light to my path, according to your word in Psalm 119:105. Let your word be established in my life today. In Jesus' name, Amen.

A Prayer for Faith—Believing Even When It Doesn't Make Sense

"Now faith is confidence in what we hope for and assurance about what we do not see."
—Hebrews 11:1, NIV

Prayer:

Lord, I declare Hebrews 11:1—my faith is the assurance of what I do not see. Even when I don't understand, I choose to trust You. I stand on 2 Corinthians 5:7—I walk by faith and not by sight. Father, strengthen my belief where doubt tries to creep in, just as the father of the demon-possessed boy cried out to Jesus in Mark 9:24: *"Lord, I believe; help my unbelief."* My faith rests not in circumstances but in You. Hebrews 12:2 says that you are the author and finisher of my faith, and I believe and trust in what it says. I choose to believe in your word and in your will. In Jesus' name, Amen.

A Prayer for Deliverance—Freedom from Addiction, Strongholds, or Fear

"So if the Son sets you free, you will be free indeed." —John 8:36, NIV

Prayer:

Jesus, I need your power to break what I can't break on my own. Whether it's a habit, a fear, a mindset, or a stronghold, I surrender it to you. I don't want to live in bondage. I want to walk in freedom. Set me free from everything that keeps me stuck. Break every chain, every lie, every cycle. Jesus, I declare John 8:36—whom the Son sets free is free indeed. Every stronghold, addiction, and spirit of fear is broken now over my life. I stand on 2 Timothy 1:7—I have not been given a spirit of fear but of power, love, and a sound mind. Chains are falling, cycles are ending, and lies of the enemy are silenced. I walk in the freedom of the Spirit that is written about in 2 Corinthians 3:17, and I claim my freedom by the blood of Jesus. Amen.

A Prayer for Family—Covering Marriage, Children, and Loved Ones

"But as for me and my household, we will serve the Lord." —Joshua 24:15, NIV

Prayer:

Father, thank you for the gift of my family. I decree Joshua 24:15 over my household—we will serve the Lord. I declare Psalm 91 over my family—angels guard us in all our ways, and no evil shall come near our dwelling. I speak Deuteronomy 28:13 over my children—they are the head and not the tail, above only and not beneath. I release peace over my marriage, unity over my home, and blessings over every generation connected to me. My family is yours, and we will serve you, Lord; we are covered by the blood of Jesus and are secured in your hands in Jesus' name. Amen.

A Prayer for Relationships—Healing Conflict, Building Trust, and Love

"Above all, love each other deeply, because love covers over a multitude of sins."
—1 Peter 4:8, NIV

Prayer:

Lord, You see every relationship in my life—the close ones, the strained ones, and the ones that need healing. Lord, I declare 1 Peter 4:8—I will love deeply, because love covers a multitude of sins. Where there has been conflict, I speak reconciliation. Where there has been offense, I release forgiveness. Your Word says in Colossians 3:14 that love binds everything together in perfect unity, so I release that love over every relationship connected to me. Teach me to be patient, to walk in grace, and to pursue peace with all men, as it's written in your word according to Hebrews 12:14. In Jesus' name, Amen.

A Prayer for Gratitude—Cultivating Thankfulness in All Circumstances

"Give thanks in all circumstances; for this is God's will for you in Christ Jesus."
—1 Thessalonians 5:18, NIV

Prayer:

God, thank you. I am grateful not only for the blessings I can see but also for the ones I've overlooked, misinterpreted, or taken for granted. Help me to see your goodness in the ordinary and to be thankful in every season. Father, I declare 1 Thessalonians 5:18—I give thanks in all circumstances, for this is Your will for me in Christ Jesus. Even in trials, I confess Romans 8:28—all things are working together for my good. I choose to see your goodness in every season and to count my blessings daily. Gratitude is my portion, and complaining has no power over me. Today, I enter your gates with thanksgiving and your courts with praise (Psalm 100:4). In Jesus' name, Amen.

A Prayer for Courage—Boldness to Step Into New Seasons and Challenges

"Have I not commanded you? Be strong and courageous. Do not be afraid; do not be discouraged, for the Lord your God will be with you wherever you go." —Joshua 1:9, NIV

Prayer:

Lord, I feel the pull toward something new, and I admit, it makes me nervous. But I won't let fear have the final say. I choose courage. I choose to trust that if you're leading me, you'll also strengthen me. Father, I declare Joshua 1:9—I will be strong and courageous, for you are with me wherever I go. I reject fear and discouragement, for 2 Timothy 1:7 says I have a spirit of power, love, and a sound mind. I step boldly into new seasons, knowing that You go before me and prepare the way according to Deuteronomy 31:8. I walk in courage, confidence, and divine boldness through Christ Jesus. Amen.

A Prayer for Renewal of the Mind: Breaking Limiting Beliefs and Lies

"Do not conform to the pattern of this world, but be transformed by the renewing of your mind..." —Romans 12:2, NIV

Prayer:

Lord, I declare Romans 12:2—my mind is renewed and transformed by Your Word. My God, I bring You my thoughts—the ones that weigh me down, limit me, or speak lies to my heart. I reject every lie of the enemy and take every thought captive to obey Christ (2 Corinthians 10:5). Replace them with your truth. Uproot every belief that doesn't line up with who you say I am. Renew my mind. Refresh my perspective. Let Philippians 4:8 guide my thoughts; help me focus on whatever is true, noble, right, pure, lovely, and praiseworthy. Let my thinking be filled with hope, faith, and freedom. Today, my mind is sharp, clear, and aligned with heaven. In Jesus' name, Amen.

A Prayer for Patience—Waiting with Trust Instead of Frustration

"The Lord is good to those whose hope is in him, to the one who seeks him; it is good to wait quietly for the salvation of the Lord."
—Lamentations 3:25–26, NIV

Prayer:

Lord, I confess—waiting is hard. My heart wants answers. My flesh wants speed. But I know that you are working in the waiting. Teach me to wait with faith instead of frustration. Father, I declare Lamentations 3:25–26—You are good to those who wait on You. I reject impatience, anxiety, and frustration. I rest in Psalm 27:14—I will wait on the Lord, be of good courage, and You will strengthen my heart. While I wait, I worship. While I wait, I trust. While I wait, I remain steadfast in faith. Your timing is perfect, and I will not be moved. In Jesus' name, Amen.

A Prayer for Justice—Seeking Fairness for the Oppressed and Voiceless

"Learn to do right; seek justice. Defend the oppressed. Take up the cause of the fatherless; plead the case of the widow."
—Isaiah 1:17, NIV

Prayer:

Righteous Judge, I declare Isaiah 1:17—I will seek justice, defend the oppressed, and stand for the voiceless. Father, I lift up those who are overlooked, unheard, and hurting. You are the God of justice—the Defender of the voiceless. Your Word says in Proverbs 21:15 that when justice is done, it brings joy to the righteous. Lord, let righteousness and justice be established in my home, my community, and my nation. Use my voice to speak truth and my hands to serve with love. Let justice roll down like waters and righteousness like a mighty stream (Amos 5:24). In Jesus' name, Amen.

A Prayer for Purpose—Discovering and Walking in Your Calling

"For we are God's handiwork, created in Christ Jesus to do good works, which God prepared in advance for us to do."
—Ephesians 2:10, NIV

Prayer:

Lord, I want to live with purpose. I want to do what you've created me to do, not to impress others, but to please you. Help me to walk in obedience, even if the steps feel small. Father, I declare Ephesians 2:10—I am Your workmanship, created in Christ Jesus for good works that You prepared in advance for me. My life has purpose. Nothing about me is an accident. I stand on Jeremiah 29:11—You know the plans; You have for me plans to prosper me and not to harm me. Order my steps into divine assignment. Let every gift, talent, and anointing in me be used for Your glory. I am aligned with my calling, and I will fulfill my purpose. In Jesus' name, Amen.

A Prayer for Humility—Resisting Pride and Walking in God's Grace

"God opposes the proud but shows favor to the humble." —James 4:6, NIV

Prayer:

Father, keep my heart low before you. I don't want pride to harden me or block what you're trying to do. Teach me to stay teachable, tender, and surrendered. Father, I declare James 4:6—I walk in humility, and Your grace is upon me. Pride, arrogance, and self-reliance will not take root in my heart. Philippians 2:3 says to do nothing out of selfish ambition but in humility value others above myself. Lord, keep me teachable, surrendered, and tender to Your Spirit. All I have comes from You, so I return the glory to You. Let me give you the glory in all things. In Jesus' name, Amen.

A Prayer for Hope—Holding On When Life Feels Hopeless or Dark

"May the God of hope fill you with all joy and peace as you trust in him, so that you may overflow with hope by the power of the Holy Spirit." —Romans 15:13, NIV

Prayer:

Lord, when life feels heavy and my heart grows weary, breathe hope into me again. Please remind me that you are not finished. Fill me with peace while I wait. Let my hope be rooted in who you are—not in what I see. I may not understand the process, but I trust the One writing the story. Lord, I declare Romans 15:13—You are the God of hope, filling me with joy and peace as I trust in You. Darkness has no power over me, for Psalm 42:11 says, *"Put your hope in God, for I will yet praise Him."* I choose hope over despair, light over darkness, and faith over fear. My future is secure in You. I overflow with hope by the power of the Holy Spirit. In Jesus' name, Amen.

A Prayer for Revival—Personal and Community Spiritual Awakening

"Will you not revive us again, that your people may rejoice in you?" —Psalm 85:6, NIV

Prayer:

Father, I declare Psalm 85:6—revive me again so I may rejoice in You. Ignite a fresh fire in my heart, my home, and my community. Joel 2:28 promises that You will pour out Your Spirit on all flesh, so I call for revival in this generation. God, let revival begin with me. Stir a fresh hunger for your Word, your presence, and your power. Let dry bones live again (Ezekiel 37:4). Let hearts be awakened, churches be renewed, and nations turn back to You. Revival begins with me, Lord—use me for Your glory. Pour out your Spirit, like rain, and breathe life into every dry place. In Jesus' name, Amen.

A Prayer for Rest—Finding Balance and Renewal in Body and Soul

"Come to me, all you who are weary and burdened, and I will give you rest."
—Matthew 11:28, NIV

Prayer:

Jesus, I bring you my tired soul. I've been running, striving, and carrying too much, and I need your rest. I declare Matthew 11:28—I come to You, and You give me rest. I lay down every burden, every stress, and every weight at your feet. Help me pause without guilt. Teach me to breathe again. Psalm 23:2 says, "You lead me beside still waters and restore my soul. " I receive your peace that surpasses all understanding. Let your peace quiet the noise around me and the weight within me. (Philippians 4:7). Your presence renews my body, mind, and spirit. I rest in You, and You sustain me. and I trust you to hold what I've been trying to carry. In Jesus' name, Amen.

A Prayer for Joy—Experiencing God's Delight Regardless of Circumstances

"You make known to me the path of life; you will fill me with joy in your presence, with eternal pleasures at your right hand."
—Psalm 16:11, NIV

Prayer:

Father, I declare Psalm 16:11 today—in Your presence, there is fullness of joy. I choose joy today, not because of circumstances, but because of who You are. Let joy rise up in my heart like a song, steady, quiet, and full of strength. Nehemiah 8:10 also says the joy of the Lord is my strength, so I receive fresh joy that strengthens me. Restore the joy of my salvation according to Psalm 51:12. Let me laugh again, celebrate again, and see goodness in even the simplest things. I choose joy. I will sing Your praises, my spirit will rejoice, and I will delight in You always. In Jesus' name, Amen.

Closing Prayer

"The Lord bless you and keep you; the Lord make His face shine upon you and be gracious to you; the Lord turn His face toward you and give you peace." —Numbers 6:24–26

Heavenly Father,

I lift up every reader who has journeyed through these pages. Let Your Word take deep root in their heart and bear much fruit. I declare Psalm 1:3 over their life—that they are like trees planted by streams of water, yielding fruit in season, their leaves never withering, and whatever they do shall prosper.

Cover their homes with peace, their families with protection, and their future with hope. Strengthen their prayer life so that every time they open their mouth to pray, Your Word flows with power, faith, and authority.

Lord, bless them and keep them, shine Your face upon them, and give them supernatural rest, joy, and favor. May their lives testify to the power of praying the Scriptures.
In Jesus' mighty name, Amen.

Personal Reflections and Prayer Notes:

Personal Reflections and Prayer Notes:

Personal Reflections and Prayer Notes:

A Note of Thanks

Dear Reader,

Thank you for walking through these pages with me. It has been an honor to share this journey of prayer with you—covering yourself and your family with God's Word, His promises, and His love.

I hope that reading this has bolstered your faith, inspired your heart, and enhanced your prayer life.

More than that, I pray you feel empowered to pray and have become confident in praying God's word back to him, confidently knowing that God Himself is partnering with you in every step.

Your time and trust mean so much to me. Every prayer spoken, every scripture declared, every journaling prompt reflected upon—these are seeds that will bear fruit in your family's lives and in your own.

If this book has blessed you, I invite you to read my other books, which were written to encourage and equip you in prayer and faith. Each one continues this mission: to draw us closer to God and to strengthen our families in His Word.

Thank you again for allowing me to be part of your prayer journey.

May the Lord bless you richly and abundantly as you continue to seek Him.

With love and gratitude,
Ramatu

About the Author

Ramatu Allen is a wife, mother of three, author and passionate encourager of women navigating life's real and raw seasons.

Born and raised in Liberia, West Africa, Ramatu brings a rich cultural heritage and deep spiritual resilience to everything she writes and teaches.

Through her personal journey of healing from parental pain, embracing forgiveness, and learning to love herself again, Ramatu has become a voice of hope for women seeking restoration and purpose.

Her words are rooted in authenticity, faith, and the belief that even broken places can bloom with grace.

She is the author of:

- West African Proverbs and Their Simple Meanings, a heartfelt celebration of cultural wisdom

- Mending the Heart: Your Path to Healing After Childhood Abandonment and Emotional Neglect. Ramatu shared her personal story of restoration and faith.

- The powerful and expanding We Must Pray series includes the following titles:

  - We Must Pray For Our Sons: A Mother's Guide to Raising Faithful, Brave and Honorable Sons Through Daily Prayers and Devotions.

  - We Must Pray For Our Daughters: A Mother's Guide to Raising Girls with Faith, Strength, and Grace Through Daily Prayers and Devotions

  - We Must Pray the Scriptures: The Life-Changing Power of Praying God's Word Over Every Area of Your Life.

During the day, Ramatu works in banking, and in the evening, she empowers women through business coaching. She helps them build smart financial habits and create healthier relationships with money by using strategies based on her personal experience with debt and her 17-plus years of banking experience.

She also mentors aspiring entrepreneurs in turning their life experiences into digital products that share their stories and generate sustainable income.

Whether through her books, prayer guides, or coaching programs, Ramatu's mission is clear:

To help women heal, rise, and thrive with faith and prayer.

She reminds every woman that her voice matters, her story holds power, and her dreams are worth the prayer.

Ramatu lives in Ohio with her loving husband and their three sons. You can connect with her on social media @ramatuallen, explore her books at www.rallenbooks.com or her coaching programs or latest projects at www.ramatuallen.com.

Also in the We Must Pray Series by Ramatu Allen

We Must Pray For Our Sons: A Mother's Guide to Raising Faithful, Brave, and Honorable Sons Through Daily Prayers and Devotions

A powerful prayer journey for mothers of boys. This heartfelt guide walks alongside you as you cover your son from infancy to manhood with wisdom, truth, and fierce faith. Includes prayers, scriptures, journaling prompts, and affirmations for every stage of a boy's life.

We Must Pray For Our Daughters: A Mother's Guide to Raising Girls with Faith, Strength, and Grace Through Daily Prayers and Devotions

This companion volume is written for mothers raising daughters in today's complex world. From friendships and confidence to purpose, protection, and faith—this book offers scriptural prayers and guidance to help your daughter become the woman God created her to be.

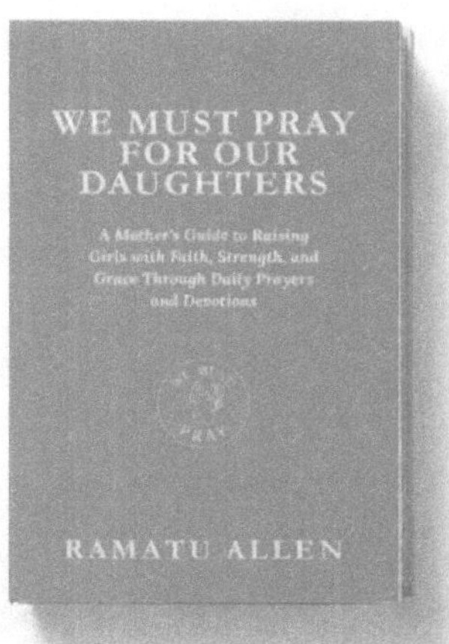

You don't have to walk this road alone. Let's continue growing together as believers who pray the Word of God with power, faith, and authority. Want to stay connected or learn about future books in the series?

Follow me on social media at @ramatuallen. Visit www.rallenbooks.com for books and www.ramatuallen.com for updates and information about my coaching programs.

Other Books

Scripture-led Journal for Praying for sons

A guided journal for healing from childhood wounds.

Mending the Heart: Your Path to Healing After Childhood Abandonment and Emotional Neglect. This book shares a story of restoration and faith.

Thank You Once More For Reading!

I pray this book has blessed, encouraged, and strengthened you in your walk with God. Writing it was a labor of love, and my greatest joy is knowing it reached your heart.

If this book has inspired you, taught you something new, or drawn you closer to the Lord, would you partner with me in spreading the message of prayer by leaving a review?

Reviews not only help others discover this book, but they also remind me that the seeds God allowed me to sow are bearing fruit.

Here's How You Can Help:

1. Go to the platform where you purchased this book.

2. Scroll down to the "Customer Reviews" section.

3. Click "Write a Review" and share a few words about how this book impacted you.

Your review doesn't have to be long or fancy—just honest. Every review helps more believers find encouragement through these pages.

Thank you for being part of this journey with me. Your support means the world to me! With love & gratitude, Ramatu Allen